One
for the Road

Published in Great Britain by Private Eye Productions Ltd.,
34 Greek Street, London W1.
In association with Andre Deutsch Ltd.,
105 Great Russell Street, London WC1.

© 1982 Pressdram Limited.

Illustrations by George Adamson, © 1982.

Designed by Martin Lee.

ISBN 23397511.

Printed by Billing & Sons Ltd. Worcester

One
for the Road

Richard Ingrams & John Wells
Illustrated by George Adamson

PRIVATE EYE/ANDRE DEUTSCH

Dear Bill,

There are times sitting upstairs when I get a bit gloomy about the way things are going. The best they can say nowadays is that it's all bottoming out, or alternatively flattening out, which means in layman's language that things couldn't possibly be worse and therefore are bound to get better.

The only gleam on the horizon has been the Major's greenhouses. I don't know if I've told you, but the old boy has been on to me for some time, usually ringing up very late at night and in an emotional condition, protesting about the cost of heating lettuces. His thinking is that no one will buy his greenhouses if the overheads are going to go straight through the ceiling the moment they turn on the juice.

I put his point of view to little Howe as he was getting into his overcoat the other morning. (Damn funny weather we've been having — Maurice Picarda woke up in a snowdrift outside the Cat & Hamster and thought he was having the DTs.) As they have this rebellion on their hands from the backwoodsmen I found a sympathetic ear. The Major's argument was that the other Euros subsidise the Small Radish Farmer with cheap Derv whilst the Men of Kent have to pay through the nose and go to the wall, result death of the British Radish Industry. Howe hummed and hahed for a bit, but I could see it was soaking in. Anyway, they've now agreed to chop 10p off their original 20p on diesel, although the mark-up on Four-Star remains the same. I don't personally see what they're all so steamed up about, 20p nowadays being about tuppence three-farthings in real money, but the MPs are a funny lot, they all feel obliged to let off steam from time to time, as does our friend the Major, and I suppose it's worth it to keep him quiet.

Meanwhile they're all fastening their seat belts and waiting for the balloon to go up yet again over Ulster. The usual scenario — chaps starving themselves to death, hooligans roving the streets, Paisley trying to garner a few votes on the sidelines with his cretinous parrot cries as usual, Boss and Whitelaw doing their two wise monkeys number over no surrender to the men of violence. I didn't say anything at the time, but personally I thought it was a mistake to allow the Vatican sky pilot Rev. McGoo to get in on the act. My experience as a rugger referee is that the best way with this class of customer is to let them stew and pay no attention. The Pope seems a decent enough cove but he's making a fundamental error in thinking there's anything you can do with a Bog Trotter once he gets the bit between his teeth. Flying in some top brass to hear the deathbed confession only makes the buggers think themselves important. I may have said this before, Bill, but quite frankly there's only one thing to do and that's for us to get the hell out of Ireland and leave the little monkeys to pelt each other with droppings in perpetuity. I have repeated this formula, ad nauseam I may say, to Ol' Oyster Eyes, but the trouble would appear to be that they signed some damnfool piece of paper a few years ago promising the Prods there would be no twitching of the rug, leaving in the lurch, etc. I said to Whitelaw this Government had torn up enough pieces of paper of that kind to fill a Corporation Rubbish Tip, so why hang about? As with the White Trash in Rhodesia, when it comes to selling people of that ilk down the river a short sharp shock is probably healthier in the long run. Gloomy shaking of the head, impression conveyed yours truly talking through hat as ever. Whitelaw knows perfectly well that I represent the voice of sanity, but he can't bring himself to face it.

On a more serious note, Maurice and I had not a bad day out at Worplesdon on Thursday and bumped into old Scatty Longmuir with that girlfriend of his who used to be some very big noise in the ATS. She got a bit tiddly at the Merry Mermaid and we had to rig up some sort of stretcher out of my Sherlock Holmes overcoat to lug her out into the carpark where she slept it off in the back of Scatty's Japanese Land-rover. Scatty has really cashed in over the last week or so with this boom in the City, and was ordering doubles like a man possessed. I did what I could to introduce a note of realism with one or two anecdotes about the Monk, but he wouldn't hear a word of it. Margaret was a wonderful woman, say what you like about this country but we could still drink the rest of the world under the table any day of the week. As we were breaking up there seemed to be some move afoot to hire a chara and come up to Town for the Royal Wedding. Number Ten an ideal base camp. I only hope that in the morning they won't have remembered anything about it.

Ah well, sun is over the yard arm, so down to work.

Yours aye,

DENIS

10 Downing Street
Whitehall

8 MAY 1981

Dear Bill,

Bit of a turn-up about old Giscard, what? Losing the election, I mean. I met him once or twice at the Common Market get-togethers, and he always struck me as a prize greaser. In my experience any Frog in office for more than a couple of years starts to think he's Napoleon or Louis the Whatever It Was, at which point the lower orders winkle out the cobblestones and create havoc. Then they bring in someone new and all go back to sipping their evil-smelling liqueurs in their pavement cafes. At which point the whole process begins all over again.

The funny thing was that nobody here knew the first thing about this Mitterand cove, and Carrington had to send out for a copy of *Paris Match* so they'd recognise him when they have to meet him. In the meantime Herr Schidt caught the first shuttle over to RAF Benson and was soon closeted with M. in the Gladstone Room plotting the Frog's downfall on the grounds that he's a Leftie. Personally, as you know, Bill, I don't trust any of them further than I can throw them, but M. loves all the toing and froing and the argy-bargy about the price of fish. I have refrained from pointing out to her that there may be some lesson to be learned from the tumbril treatment being meted out to old Giscard, though I like to think that with yours truly in the wings exercising a restraining influence this scenario may be avoided.

Trouble is, so long as old Worzel Gummidge remains nominally in charge of Transport House, M. very naturally feels she's got Downing Street on a long lease. Even their modest successes in the Local Elections have only led to further feuding, hair-pulling, nose-thumbing, etc, and I gather that relations between Brothers Foot and Benn have now degenerated to total non-speaks. Though I must say, Bill, barmy though he is, old Wedgie of the Whirling Eyes does occasionally hole in one, viz his scheme for getting the hell out of Ulster a.s.a.p. I don't know whether he got the idea through the odd political by-ways from yours truly, but I have observed over the years that lunatics do have moments of clarity. Do you remember when the Major's father had to be incarcerated at Esher wearing that funny life-jacket with the ribbons at the back, he still managed to pick out the first three in the St Leger when the rest of us lost our shirts.

Needless to say, the moment poor old Benn comes out with something rational for the first time in years they all come down on him like a ton of bricks. Not that I'd go along with the scheme for dropping in U Thant and the Blue Berets to keep order on the Bogside. It was always my experience as a referee that there are certain fixtures best left unsupervised. All either side wants to do is tear the other lot limb from limb and the presence of a fellow in black blowing a whistle only brings discredit on the Referees' Association.

I pointed this out to little Atkins, Our Man in Belfast, who toddled round to be given his Battle Orders by the Boss. If you ask me the poor sod is fast cracking up under the strain, and like certain other members of M's entourage who shall remain nameless has none too strong a head for the Red

Infuriator. Personally I think the solution to all our troubles would be to send the Monk over there, if only because he's used to having things hurled at him by yobs of all shapes and sizes every time he emerges from his limo. He's apparently made an absolute balls-up of the Industrial Brief, and when it comes to foaming at the mouth he, Paisley and Enoch would make a wonderful threesome.

I managed to escape from Colditz for a sharpener or twain with the Major at the RAC Club on Tuesday. He had come up to sell some old lengths of garden hose at Sotheby's, and we ran into Sticky Wilkinson, who is now working there as their expert on Japanese Ceramics, would you believe it? Sticky and the Major went very much off the deep end about the Hunger Strikers, but I did offer one ray of hope, which is that in my experience when the Proprietor puts her foot down in a big way at the Bar of World Opinion, stressing that there will be no last-minute reprieves, U-Turns, etc, it is quite often a sign that she is on the verge of going about, though of course this is never admitted afterwards.

I remember something of the kind happening with Daphne when she refused to have that Antiques woman of Picarda's in the house ever again after the incident at the Flower Festival, and then, blow me, there they were two weeks later closeted in the snug at the Goat & Compasses, swapping dirty limericks, shrieking with laughter, and thick as thieves over a couple of large ones. I seem to recall Maurice got a snap of them, albeit rather blurred.

Apparently there are some Jap reject clubs on offer at Lillywhites. If Daphne persists in her New York trip, you could hop on the Bluebell Line and we could get together over a spot of lunch at the Club.

Yours as ever,

DENIS

10 Downing Street
Whitehall
22 MAY 1981

Dear Bill,

Terrible weather we've been having! Boris says it's caused by the US Space Shuttle. You probably heard about my disastrous little outing with the Major and his new friend from the North. I don't know if you've met him yet, but he's called Bagley and runs a fish farm somewhere outside Newcastle. We got down to Worplesdon at opening time, to find the course completely waterlogged and the Club Secretary in his waders behind the bar v. apologetic, cellar flooded, no booze but he had got this new Space Invaders machine in, would we like to try our luck free of charge? Not much of a consolation, you might think, Bill, but the Major had fortunately come equipped for emergencies with a crate of Auld MacTavish Highland Dew tucked away in the boot of his Jag, and after a snort of twain I got rather gripped by the machine. Have you seen one in your peregrinations? You put in fifty p. and suddenly the screen is filled with rank upon rank of nasty little foreign jobs advancing on a broad front. Then you press the tit and blow them up. It doesn't sound much, but it's damn clever the way they do it, and by three o'clock in the afternoon I was really beginning to get the hang of things. By that time however the Major and his friend were getting a bit peckish and persuaded me to join them at a local hostelry just down the road called the Golden Bucket. They didn't seem particularly pleased when Mine Host told us that the kitchen was shut and slammed the door on Bagley's fingers when he tried to use the phone to place a bet on the 3.45 at Haydock Park.

We then drove into Bagshot. I'd forgotten what a dump that place is, Bill. All bypasses and Shopping Centres, not an afternoon drinking club in sight. In the end we had to make do with what are called Club Sandwiches at some ghastly Playboy Hotel. £4.99 for two bits of dried toast, a handful of crisps, an old bit of turkey and an olive on a stick. However, as luck would have it, they had another Space Invaders machine of slightly different design, this time with little orange lawn-mowers wobbling in from outer space and very satisfactory sound effects when they blew up. The Major said he didn't want to play because it reminded him of the time he had to go into that clinic at Cheltenham with Delirium Tremens. Rain still bucketing down, Bagley getting legless on Southern Comfort, so we decided to drop in on Maurice Picarda's brother, who breeds Dobermanns outside Dorking. By this time Bagley had seized the wheel. As you know, Bill, map-reading has always been my forte, but the Major like a bloody fool insisted on holding the book upside down, swearing he knew the way, and ticking Bagley off about not overtaking. Old Bill fell in behind just as we were going past Guildford Cathedral and from then on it was like American television.

When they finally ran us off the road, Bagley made the serious error in my view of breathing in Mr Plod's face and asking him did he realise who he'd got in the front seat, and that we were already late for a vital rencontre with the Boss. Absolutely fatal, Bill. Much ironical banter from the Force, comrade Bagley frog-marched off to the Station to give a sample, the Major and myself bundled into the back seat of the Panda with no great civility. On arrival at the nick I was delighted to see that they had one of the Space Invader machines, which had apparently fallen off the back of a lorry, this time with submarines which blew up with a puff of green smoke. And so I passed the time quite agreeably while Bagley was roughed up in the cells in the usual manner. We finally got out with a severe caution at midnight — I think the Major had made some contribution to the Christmas Fund — and travelled back hard arse in a very slow train to Charing Cross.

So much for politics. The Boss has been over in Belfast waving the flag and boosting morale among the troops. A great mistake, in my view. Suggesting the Maze is some sort of plush holiday camp is not going to get her anywhere with Haughey and his mob, and she would have been much better employed getting them all prepared to have the rug pulled from under their muddy boots and left to retreat to the mountain-tops with Paisley and his Merry Men in Black. When she got back she was v. cock-a-hoop on account of one of the SAS sports having bagged a brace of troublemakers the day before. I made the point that it was a bit like the Space Invaders. You can knock off two or even two hundred, but the little buggers still keep coming on. Unhappily, this pointful little parable was less than well received. Boss not familiar with machines and clearly thought I was due for a spell at the Cheltenham Clinic (see above).

Ah me, plans now afoot for the Wedding. I think I have a scheme for avoiding it altogether. Poor old barmy Fothergill is mad keen to go, and I thought given a pair of my specs and the Sherlock Holmes coat he might well pass undetected. Yours till then,

DENIS

10 Downing Street
Whitehall
5 JUNE 1981

Dear Bill,

I was very upset to hear about your failing to make your date at the RAC with Maurice last Tuesday due to the traffic jams. I don't know if you realised that the whole snarl-up was caused by the arrival of the Chief Wog and his retinue of wives, slaves, eunuchs etc. If you had, I imagine you would have been even more hopping mad than you were. Carrington, poor little sod, was in a state of blue funk as the C.W. has a way of taking umbrage at the drop of a hat, and as you may remember there was no end of a hooha a couple of years back when he took exception to something on Nationwide. Ever since then the FO have been pursuing what you and I would call a brown tongue policy vis a vis our friends in the black tents, crafty little buggers that they are.

I myself was on an eight-line whip from the Boss about not putting my foot in it, no reference to members being amputated for fornication, stay off booze etc. Hence my mild surprise, once the evil-smelling tide had surged in to Number Ten for the official pow-wow, robes billowing and dishcloths awry, to be taken on one side by one of their number, obviously some relative of Old Sheepseyes himself — a wizened little geezer with silver teeth who introduced himself as Prince Big Ben Arafat or something of that sort. (Just imagine, Bill, if the Duke of Edinburgh was allowed to have as many wives as

he liked, wherever you went you'd be stumbling over Prince-lings on both sides of the bar in any village hostelry.) I couldn't make out what he was saying at first, and was about to summon the interpreter, when the word "snifter" clearly emerged from the otherwise unintelligible harangue, closely followed by "snort" and "gorblimey".

The Boss was deep in parleyvoo with His Eminence, but Boris, who has some experience of Russian involvement in the Middle East, quickly assessed the situation and beckoned us through to his little pantry where I was somewhat surprised to see several teapots already laid out. There was soon quite a party in progress, with the Sons of the Desert knocking back Boris's powerful snorterinos out of English bone china as to the manner born. Boris himself meanwhile emphasised on behalf of the Government Margaret's deep sense of shock and outrage at Mr Begin's latest brainstorm in Iraq. I couldn't quite make this out, because when M. and Carrington were chewing it over during breakfast they both agreed that it was high time someone gave the Iraqi a bloody nose, serve him damn well right. However I held my peace.

An expedition to the Playboy Club had just been proposed by one of the Sheiks, when the Boss clearly realised the Royal Entourage had thinned out a bit, and swept in like Matron into a midnight feast, clapping her hands and shooing them through into the Blue Conference Room for the usual nausea and exchange of official speeches. At dinner I myself was clamped between two very orthodox ones, who were sipping rancid goat's milk and clearing their throats a good deal. As you know Bill, if people neither drink nor play golf I always find the going rather hard, but if you remember Sidi Birani as I do, it is a bit humiliating to see the tables so entirely turned, British bankers cap in hand to Brother Wog for a few million for the price of a snort etc.

The weird thing about it, Bill, as I tried to explain to Carrington, is that this little local difficulty the Boss has got herself into over the Falling Pound etc. as far as I can see is all the fault of the Chief Wog doing what we asked him for a change. Keep down the price of oil, we cry, little fellow does so, whole economy topples. Economics has never been my strong suit, as you know, Bill, but Boris explained it to me as he was mopping up after the visit. If they keep down the price of oil, our trickle from the North Sea goes down too, whereupon all the sharks and money-lenders to whom we are in hock immediately close in, grab everything there is to be grabbed and bugger off to America, where Hopalong is making conditions particularly nice for them. Pound sinks, inflation up, Boss left chewing fingernails through the slow watches of the night.

I told her that Maurice was over the moon about the cheaper pound, as it means Picwarmth should be able to shift a whole lot of double glazing that has been gathering dust down in that warehouse of his at Sevenoaks and load it off on the Swiss who are, so he says, crying out for it: what was good for Maurice was good for the country. Boss however not convinced and she has now summoned a grand conflab of Monetarists so that she can tell them where they went wrong. My main worry is how does this leave my deposit account at the Nat-West. According to Furniss, their rate of interest is bound to go up again, so that can't be bad. On the other hand if Daphne insists on going over with her hairdresser to get mugged in Miami you must warn her that she's going to be paying through the nose for her creature comforts and that Sidmouth might be a better bet in the circs.

Barmy.Fothergill is chuffed to Naafibreaks about being sent along to the Wedding in my stead, so keep your fingers crossed for a night on the tiles.

DENIS

10 Downing Street
Whitehall
19 JUNE 1981

Dear Bill,
I don't know if you've been been watching the tennis. I find it all a bit depressing. You settle down with a snort in your hand on a sunny afternoon, expecting to hear nothing but the thwock of ball on gut, the occasional cry of the umpire and the rustle of applause as you drift away into a deep sleep, and

all you get is one or other of these superbrats effing and blinding at the authorities like Question Time in the House of Commons. Admittedly all those linesmen are geriatrics. Squiffy's brother did it for years and years, died in harness, and was, I think, still upright in his little chair for several hours before they discovered he'd passed on. But none of that excuses intemperance from the young. Besides which it now emerges that most of the women are ferocious lezzies, and that no young girl is safe in the showers. All of which rather takes the gloss off the whole caboodle. Thank heavens the world of golf is not infested with perverts. (Though it has to be said that from time to time life down at Worplesdon gets pretty hairy when the ex-Battle of Britain ace Banger Perkins blows his top and starts thrashing the caddies with his niblick.)

Back at the Bunker, the casual observer might surmise that the old girl's hair would be falling out by now, fingernails gnawed to the knuckle, future viewed with despair. Not so. Constant pop of champagne corks, flushed faces and cackles of lunatic laughter. As you may have seen, she summoned all her Wets in for a dressing-down a week or so ago. I collared Carrington on the way out, beckoning him into the Snug with a bottle of Old Grand-dad, to which I happen to know he is not averse, and received a very amusing account of how things had fallen out.

To begin with, the Monk, who was looking pale, made a solemn announcement that he couldn't be at the next meeting because he had to go into "hospital". Needless to say, much sniggering up sleeves, assumed by all and sundry "hospital" = funny farm, crunch come at last, etc. Sensing this, Sir Keith added a rider to the effect that he had in fact ruptured himself — no laughing matter I can tell you after my own experiment in waterskiing in 1954 — but there was a good deal of tittering, noseblowing, eyewiping, etc, before the Boss moved them on to Any Further Business. Once again the revolt of the Wets, which had been built up as another Battle of the Bulge, failed to materialise, Farmer Prior making a few half-hearted remarks about the need to help school-leavers, for which he was savaged by M. and told he hadn't got a monopoly on concern and compassion. Then they were all ordered to go away and think up some more cuts, at which there was a groan, scraping of chairs, and that was that...

Next thing was that M. had to go down to the Circus Maximus to do battle with old Worzelus Gummidgus, the

white-locked champion of the Plebs who, armed with the new unemployment figures, clearly scented blood. According to Boris, who was in the Distinguished Strangers Gallery, Worzel did his usual knock-about turn, roars of ribaldry from the Smelly Socks Brigade, much coming and going from the bar, cries of Resign! etc, whereupon the Boss weighed in like Queen Boudicca of yore, scimitars flashing at the hub-caps, and cut them all to ribbons. Poor old Worzel was soundly reprimanded for making jokes about a tragedy over which she had no control, and the old boy staggered off into the night muttering under his breath.

I caught sight of him the other day, at a reception given for Mr Yamaha, Leader of the Nips, and he looked to me very much below par. I think they all hoped that once Benn had been carried off to the Intensive Care Unit with straws in his hair he would be out of action for the duration. Now he's bouncing back with eyes rotating even faster than before and giving them all pause for thought. Incidentally, according to Dr O'Moynihan, pains in the legs are the result of drinking too much tea. Which only goes to show, Bill, that all Eric my bodyguard says about how snorts burn out the brain cells is all absolute cock, and you're far worse off knocking back the Typhoo with the Yobs like poor old Wedgie B. Needless to say, a lot of the Trots are now firmly convinced that the CIA shot a poisoned dart into his bum through a furled umbrella as he was coming out of the Public Library, but if they did, more power to their elbow and one can only pray that they will persevere in their efforts.

Meanwhile in Warrington, old Fatcat Jenkins is fighting a lone battle for the SDP. The *Telegraph* seems to have taken quite a shine to him, and, hoping to pour oil on the troublous tide, I took the liberty of opining at breakfast that he might well do us a bit of good up in the Northern Darkness by buggering up the Reds. To my surprise, I got my head bitten off in no uncertain manner. We live, I was told, in a two-party state, Worzel not such a bad chap, no need for opportunists to come into Croydon North-West and overturn the applecart.

I may have said this before, Bill, but I sometimes find it hard to follow the reasoning of the politicos, though Carrington is pretty sound on this Begin bugger. If he has his way we'll all be blown into the middle of next week. Talking of which, will you be free at all to entertain some of Picarda's Common Market customers for a day out with the clubs at Richmond? It could apparently be the big breakthrough for Picwarmth. After he got the bum's rush from the Swiss, things have been looking darkish at his Hendon headquarters over the betting shop, bank manager tapping on the frosted glass, etc, so I feel it's time for all his chums to rally round.

Till then, au reservoir,

Yrs,

DENIS

10 Downing Street

Whitehall

3 JULY 1981

Dear Bill,

Is that little bungalow at Bells Yew Green still on the market? With things as they are, I have been thinking more and more of going to ground, at least until the present riot season blows itself out. I don't know how things have been down in your neck of the woods, but up here every yob and skinhead who can find his way out of his own front door unassisted has been out in the streets lobbing bricks at the Constabulary and setting fire to the supermarkets. We're all being told to say that there's nothing racial about it, but you can't help noticing the odd coon in amongst them. Needless to say, the I Told You So Brigade has not been slow off the mark. Enoch, for whom I had a certain amount of time at one point, has been going round muttering about the Coming Apocalypse. What everyone conveniently forgets about Old Catseyes, or so Fatty Soames tells me, is that he was responsible for admitting the Minstrels in such numbers in the first place when he was Minister of Health and short of bods to swab down the Outpatients and keep the Tubes running on time. And, quite honestly, Bill, a very good job they do. I remember when poor old Maurice cracked his head open playing Torpedoes with the Battle of Britain contingent — his life was saved by a buxom Barbadian nurse called Winifred, with whom he ended up the staunchest of chums.

Meanwhile our Sailorboy Friend with the blue rinse has clearly sensed that the time has come for a coup. He was off sick for a long time, I don't know if you saw, something to do with his glands, medico apparently told him if he didn't stop signing books he was a goner. He has now come bouncing back, looking bronzed and fit, raring for a final shoot-out with M. First whiff of a Molotov Cocktail and out he pounces on the Jimmy Young Show, blaming the troubles in Toxteth, Moss Side and any other Side you care to mention on the Boss. If it wasn't for her, says our leathery-faced organist, there would be no unemployment, inflation would be down to zero, land flowing with milk and honey. All of which may be true, Bill, but it's a bit strong coming from an old stumblebum like Heath who brought the whole damn country grinding to a halt. You may remember that afternoon when all the lights went out in the Flamingo Club. But enough said.

Whitelaw to my mind is completely out of his depth. Place going up in flames all about him, and all he can suggest is that parents should be held responsible for the fifty p into the swear box the beaks are doling out by way of fines. A fat lot of good that will do. If you remember, Bill, in the old days, when the mob went on the rampage in our Protectorates, the routine was all laid down in black and white in Company Orders under Duties in Aid of the Civil Power. Select ringleader, one warning through the megaphone, and, if that failed, let fly at said ringleader with every weapon in the armory. Instead of which poor old Willie can only burble on about reinforcing their truncheons and putting blotting paper inside their helmets. I must say, Bill, if you or I was a copper lying in hospital with a fractured skull the sight of Old Oystereyes looming up at the end of the bed bringing words of comfort and joy from the Boss would not necessarily do all that much for one's morale.

On top of everything Humpty Dumpty Thorneycroft has been teetering about saying the NatWest is about to start bouncing our cheques. Party can't afford to pay the bill for Saatchi and Saatchi any more. I said that was a bloody good thing, and the sooner we see the back of those two greasy little wops with their damnfool ideas for publicity stunts the better for all of us. However with Alberto and Luigi swanking to their other advertising friends about how they run the country I don't think it will be as easy as that.

Oh, I almost forgot. That frightful ass Lord Margolis or whatever he's called has ensnared the Boss for another summer jaunt to mow down the grouse on the Isle of Muck. Do you think that crooked osteopath of Sticky's in St John's Wood could furnish me with some kind of chitty diagnosing terminal Hammer Toes or something of that nature? The Boss probably won't swallow it, but these are desperate days and it might be worth a try.

Yours under the weather,

DENIS

10 Downing Street
Whitehall
17 JULY 1981

Dear Bill,

Ah me. The best laid plans of mice and men, as the Major's mother used to say, always get ballsed up in the end. You remember my little wheeze to shunt poor old Barmy Fothergill into my slot at the Royal Wedding? Blow me if the rotten sod doesn't disappear into the Intensive Care with yet another liver attack two days before the shindig, God rot his socks, leaving yours truly with no alternative but to go down to Moss Bros and get fitted out with the grey topper and spats. As usual it proved impossible to find a native to run a tape measure over one. As you know, I have a profound aversion to any darkie or Iranian student fumbling up and down one's trouser leg. Anyway, after two hours waiting with a crowd of sambos, chinks and every other of the 57 varieties

hiring medals by the barrowload for the great day, I finally got palmed off with a suit four sizes too small and a hat that slipped down over the ears every time I cleared my throat.

Got back to the Talking Shop to find all hell had been let loose on account of the King of Spain chucking at the last minute. All because the Happy Couple, it transpires, had been routed through Gib by the FO as part of their Mediterranean Cruise. Always a pleasure to see Carrington caught with his trousers down. Obviously none of his merry band of Pinkos and Bertie Wooftahs had thought twice about it and he's now being pissed on from a great height by HRH, not to mention the reptilian chorus from the Gutter Press. As I told Carrington, who was in the process of being carpeted by the Boss, what on earth did it matter if there was one King the less in the front pew, and anyway why should C and D have all their plans changed by some little waiter figure on the Costa Brava when the apes had been on the Rock for thousands of years and are determined to remain British come what may?

After this, old cemetery-face Gilmour was wheeled on in the House to repeat my sentiments. You could tell his heart wasn't in it, Bill. He is, as you know, dripping Wet, and no doubt wants to give away every scrap of Empire that remains to any tinpot potentate that asks for it.

The Boss has come back full of beans from her little summit jaunt to Ottawa. Did you see them on the TV, Bill? Driving round in golf carts. I thought it looked bloody silly. Probably something Saatchis had thought up. The whole scenario outlined to Margaret before take-off was that the Euros should form a solid phalanx and tell Hopalong in no uncertain manner where he got off as far as Interest Rates were concerned. However, according to Boris, who went along, M. broke ranks and went completely overboard for the old screen idol, dewy-eyed assurances, sun shone out of his arse, best thing since sliced bread, etc, exact re-run of our last disastrous visit to Washington when we had to drink all those awful Bullfrogs and Rimshots or whatever they call their fancy snorts.

One odd thing, Bill. I was flicking about during her absence with my remote control job while slumped in front of the British Open, when who should pop up on the screen, looking forty years younger and not a whit more intelligent, than old Hopalong himself, holding hands with a chimpanzee while some blonde bombshell ran her fingers through his Brylcreem. Thought for a moment I might have been over-indulging, but Eric who is something of a film buff recognised it as a bit of some eighth-rate movie made to entertain the troops during the Ardennes Offensive. Very weird, nonetheless. I may have said this before, Bill, but you or I would think it jolly odd if old Wilfred Hyde White was installed at Number Ten, red buttons to hand.

They're still a bit windy, by the way, about the Fat Cat Jenkins nearly pulling it off up at Warrington. I had to sit up with the Boss to see the results on the telly and that funny little Canadian cove who's always brought on with his pendulum got quite carried away, predicting that if this sort of thing went on at the next election M's lot would be reduced to a party of one. (He didn't say who, but my guess would be Enoch.) Boss went pretty white at that, and I had to toddle off to the sherbet cupboard and administer a stiff brownie and water before the old light returned to her eyes. Since then, the Wets have been setting up even more of a caterwauling than usual, calling for U-Turns on every front if all is not to be lost, and the Proprietor had to go down and read the Riot Act to the 1922 Committee, telling them that if they'd followed her this far up shit creek it's a long way to walk back and trying to cheer them up with the news that Benn was back from hospital and once again kicking the stuffing out of old Worzel.

My account of the nuptials must wait for my next screed, Boris having just opened what looks like a very acceptable consignment of Damson Vodka from the Kremlin.

Chin chin, old fruit, and Dosvidanye.

Whoops,

DENIS

Dear Bill,

I'm sorry I missed you in all the confusion after the Nuptials. I had assumed that once we got out of St Paul's I'd be free to join you for a few celebratory tinctures in the Cat & Hamster, but not a bit of it. I was immediately shanghaied back to the Talking Shop to pass around the peanuts for every conceivable coon and dervish in creation, not to mention Mrs Hopalong, who was obviously pretty miffed at being put in Row H, while that other film star woman Grace Kelly who married the Casino fellow was right up at the front.

I don't know if you saw the ceremony on the box, Bill? All very well, no doubt, slumped at home, snort in hand, but from where I was sitting it was like being inside one of the Major's Japanese greenhouses. Frightful stench of scent, cameras poking out of every bunch of flowers, that prize ass Runcie mincing about in a silver reachmedown like something out of Dr Who, and then, to cap it all, up gets this dusky songstress from Down Under in a multicoloured tablecloth and air hostess's hat, and warbles on for bloody hours. Poor old Spencer looked a bit groggy. It was obviously touch and go whether he'd keel over bang in the middle of it like that very fat waiter did when the Major's mother was giving her song recital in Aid of the Pit Ponies.

Anyway, the Captains and the Kings have now departed, thank God, except for one poor coon who had his whole bloody country pulled from under him during the celebrations. Margaret very decently offered the SAS, in the form of two balaclava bruisers from the Prince's Gate show, to pop over there on a scheduled flight and release one of his wives who had been kidnapped. I detected a rather wistful look on the little fellow's face when he was given the glad tidings that all was well again.

Back at home a bit of excitement has blown up over the question of reshuffling Humpty Dumpty. M. had just put a cloth over the parrots' cage and was hoping to slip away for a few days of P and Q in the West Country when old Thorneycroft. God rot his socks, pops up again and starts sounding off

about poor little Howe, cheered on by Brother Pym.

It all began when Howe, hoping to rally the rabble, announced yet again that the worst was over, light at the end of the tunnel, everyone bottoming out all over the place etc. Old Humpty, as you may know, has a finger in various pies, including Sir Charles Whatsisname, the little wop with the moustache who runs the hotel chain, and they're all very worried about what the slump is doing to their profits. Humpty's tail fairly vigorously twisted in boardroom, sets up inevitable caterwauling, seeing his pension schemes jeopardised by the Boss's madcap capers.

Anyway, it didn't go down at all well with M. This isn't the first time Old Humpty's stepped out of line. Howe's talkative wife on the blower morning noon and night saying Geoffrey's been made to look a BF etc, and the word now is that Humpty is up for the one-way ticket to Siberia, possibly accompanied by Brother Pym, explanation to the faithful to suggest senility, insanity, etc. After all, he is 72, and has never struck me as being all there at the best of times. There's always a chap like that in every boardroom, burbling away into the blotting paper with no one taking a blind bit of notice.

That slimy little creep Heseltine seems to be riding high up in Liverpool. Picarda got very excited when he saw him chauffeuring a lot of fat cats round the black spots, offering them cheap sites and generous incentives. Could I put in a word for Picwarmth? He could guarantee jobs for at least half a dozen young darkies in unpaid apprentice situations making double glazing units, given suitable subsidies from HMG. I went so far as to ring up the oily little blighter on behalf of our mutual friend, only to be told that the PR exercise had finished at midnight the night before, and that anyway the Big City mob had got it all sewn up, and that this was no place for cowboys and spivs, clearly a reference to our friend. I don't mind telling you I returned the compliment on Maurice's behalf with knobs on. Give me Humpty Dumpty any day if the alternative is young Gingernuts.

I expect you saw the Son and Heir took a tumble on the Nuremberg Ring. Serve the little bugger right is all I say. I was once again urged to use my paternal influence and persuade him to set up in a small way in New Zealand, but I politely declined After all, he is nearly thirty and if he wants to go to hell in a high-speed handcart it's his bloody look-out.

I hope that doesn't sound callous, Bill, but that's the way I look at it. At least we appear to have wangled our way out of the Isle of Muck. It seems Old Pucefeatures did himself a mischief in a mantrap coming home with his ferrets and is laid up' on a bed of pain. I suppose we must be grateful for small mercies.

Yours till the sun shines,

DENIS

10 Downing Street

Whitehall

14 AUGUST 1981

Dear Bill,

I hope you got my p. c. from Bude. Rather an old joke, but I liked the surgeon's face. A look of old Groggy Rossiter about him, I thought. The weather was pretty decent on the whole, but I must say I never thought I'd heave a sigh of relief to be back at the Talking Shop.

The real nigger in the woodpile was little Peter Carrington, who managed somehow to impress tactfully on the Boss that if she didn't put her feet up and have a "real rest" she'd be following the Monk into the Bin. Hence the quiet Cornish venue, out-of-the-way bungalow, billed as being within minutes of the beach. (True, were one at the controls of Concorde.)

Boss had also decided, on the advice of the Saatchi Bros, to immerse herself in culture. You can imagine how my heart leapt to see that she had packed a fat book, called The Brothers Kamarazov, by one of those foreign birds. A good solid two thousand pages, I estimated, should allow yours truly a few days out on the links plus the odd evening off sampling the local scrumpy. All boded well on Day One. 8am, reptiles admitted for photo call, M. and I driven down to beach for surprise encounter with some old bag from Margaret's past. I refused to roll my trousers up or put a handkerchief on my head as requested by one of the guttersnipes. After that they buggered off and we were dropped back at the Bothy and left to our own devices.

Set up the deckchair for M. on the lawn, canvas stool to accommodate Prime Ministerial legs, rug in case of clouding over later in the day, Brothers Whatdyoumacallit open at page 1, step into golfing pumps and hightail it up the tracks to adjacent Clubhouse, where who should I find ensconced behind the *D. Tel.* but Harry Collis-Browne, the Major's friend from Folkestone, who made a mint out of rubber inflatables and then retired with his secretary to Godalming. Not a bad hat, by any means, and a fund of anecdote and reminiscence. All the drinks on him, not allowed to put my hand in my pocket, keen fan of the Boss, she should have Humpty Dumpty strung up by his thumbs, couldn't understand why the police weren't issued with sten guns, i.e. absolutely one of us.

Following our liquid lunch, he agreed to totter round the greens with me, and after a somewhat erratic start we produced some very remarkable golf. Somewhere about the fifteenth, Collis-Browne was just rooting about in a thicket for some temporarily lost balls when a merry "Coo-ee" brought us to our senses in no uncertain manner. I looked up, and there was the Boss, sensible shoes and hair tossed in the wind, striding across the sward knocking the tops off the dandelions with a knobbly walking stick. Hauled C-B out of the gorse bush by his braces and effected an introduction, but the old boy was a bit tongue-tied. M said to carry on, she didn't want to spoil our fun, etc, but C-B now very much off his stroke and broke three clubs before we decided to call it a day.

Boss undeterred. Suggests a pot of tea for three at Clubhouse. C-B's face falls several hundred feet, assuming a somewhat Gilmour-like mien, cove behind the bar taps side of his nose, whole scene a bit like one of those drawings they used to have before the war in *Punch* where the chap lights his cigar before the Archbishop of Canterbury. Frightfully good. Didn't Sticky W. used to have a coloured print of it in the bog? Be that as it may, we were soon grouped round a pot of well-stewed Tetley Teabags and some rather soggy toast, listening to M's resume of the Brothers K. It turned out she had devoured it at a gulp and was now redecorating the bungalow. Brothers K. apparently a let-down, not a patch on Murder Up The Nile.

Rather disastrously, old Collis-B. began to nod off during

M's opening salvoes, but I explained that he'd been badly shot up at Dunkirk and was subject to fits. M. swallowed this one. Why didn't we walk into Polperro along the cliffs? With more geographical knowledge at my disposal I might have told her, but off we set. Boss leading the way, scrawny gorse underfoot, no discernible path, wind up to gale force, sky purples over, Boss bright of eye as ever, wasn't it bracing? Three and a half hours later we encounter bewildered rustic. Turns out we are heading in wrong direction. Recover breath sufficiently to enquire whether any hostelry within reach. No, says B. R. but Golf Club over brow of hill. Discover old C-B just coming to, and ready for the first snort of the evening, clearly convinced that the Boss is some kind of spectre. Return to bungalow and spend remainder of weekend re-roofing shed, digging garden, moving rockery and installing D-I-Y double glazing which arrived unexpectedly courtesy of Picwarmth. All the bits turned out to be the wrong size, and we learn today that owners of bungalow have placed matter in hands of their solicitor.

M. is now warming up for one of her reshuffles, one scheme under consideration being to send Prior over to Northern Ireland, on the principle that if he can't stand up to the Reds let him have a crack at standing up to the IRA. Just the sort of idea you'd expect from Saatchi and Saatchi. Humpty Dumpty is definitely for the chop, having well and truly cooked his goose, and rumours are rife that some unpleasantness is in store for Fatty S. of Rhodesia fame, though what he can have done to blot his copy-book I cannot for the life of me imagine. Burning the candle at both ends again I can only assume. They're obviously going to have to find someone to sit in the Chairman's seat. I suppose you wouldn't be interested? Not over-taxing and some perks. Or perhaps that stockbroker fellow from Ferring who always pops up on the board of Maurice's companies. Lord or Bart or something. Looks good on the writing paper, inspires confidence etc. And by God, could we do with it.

Yours till Hell freezes over, i.e. any minute,

DENIS

Dear Bill,

Do you remember a year or two, following my funny turn at Thorpeness, M. sent me off to Dr O'Mingus, the little Irish quack in Folkestone, hoping that I would be ordered onto the water waggon on pain of death? I myself was in some trepidation, particularly after my second nasty blackout and an attack of total amnesia following a night on the tiles with Maurice and his lady friend from the Antique Hypermarket. Little O'Mingus drew off the normal specimens of sundry fluids, peered at them knowingly in the light, and by the way his hands shook as he held the phial it struck me he should be the one undergoing the humiliating experience rather than yours truly. Much clucking and rolling of the eyes, samples despatched, and after two or three days of agonising suspense, he came on the line to Downing Street with the All Clear, i.e. that it was perfectly in order for me to take the occasional glass of wine with my evening meal, but not to overdo it and definitely no spirits. Knowing the way these chaps exaggerate I took it as the green light, full speed ahead. And since then, I must say, everything has been ticketyboo, apart of course from the one night at the Rotary, but I blame that on the food. They should never have got that Filipino Chef in.

Be that as it may. Bugger me, come last Monday, if some honest citizen of Leicestershire, taking his dog for a walk across the rubbish tip, chances upon a cache of Top Secret Bumf, containing for starters intimate notes with regard to Yours Truly, to wit average intake of alcohol per microsecond, frequency of nocturnal perambulations, and other matters too delicate even for your hardened sensibilities. Not only my file, Bill, as it turns out, but wads of it: showbiz johnnies, the Royalty, even that nice little Oaksey man who writes the Racing Notes in the *Telegraph*, who I think we bumped into at Plumpton the day the Major had the cert. Instantly blown up out of all proportion, I need hardly add, by the waiting Reptiles. It turns out that every doctor in the country with that kind of clientele has been sending his specimens in to a Harley Street clinic where they have been pored over by some bespectacled woman who is clearly making a very good living out of it. (Odd thing, Bill, is why the Leicestershire walker happened to be the son of a journalist, and why the bespectacled woman's husband happens to be a leering PR man with some bogus Russian handle to his name. 'Nuff said.)

Meanwhile we had to do our stint with the Royalty up at Castle O'Doom. Usual palaver, luckily Runcie not there this year, a pair of coon ambassadors, a smarmy Yank or twain, and a frightful little jumped up smoothie from Newbury who has the care of the Royal Horseflesh. (He gave me a tip for the 4.30 at Redcar the afternoon he left and the damn thing died as the jockey was mounting it.) The only bit of excitement came prior to Church Parade on the Sunday morning, when the wee Kirk was invaded by the hoi polloi from all over the country, women with fat legs and wrinkly stockings come in charabancs from as far afield as Chorleywood and Rickmansworth to view the Happy Young Pair As Seen On TV. I was told to keep well in the background, but I still got a bit of a cheer from one old bag who thought I was Lord Spencer. I suppose we have got a certain amount in common.

I can't say, on the occasion I found myself next to Little Di at lunch, that I found all that much to talk to her about, but she's a perfectly decent girl, not unlike the rather daft daughter of Heatherington's who sold make-up for Elizabeth Arden in Eastbourne. The Prince, on the other hand, I found a bit of a pill. One minute ganging up with his old man in taking the mickey, a lot of bloody silly Goon Show jokes, flicking my tie out and so forth, telling the butler I was strictly teetotal and to be brought constant supplies of Perrier water — much sniggering behind doors at this — and then the next minute being deadly serious trying to spell the simplest word during the Scrabble Ordeal with Ma'am. Quite frankly I was damn glad to see the back of them.

By the time this reaches you, M. should have blown the gaff on her Shuffle. I am being kept in the dark, needless to say, but my own advice was Broadmoor for the Monk, the Senior Citizens' Eventide Home for Hailsham, and Humpty Dumpty for the firing squad. Anyway, whatever M. may have on her plate, it is nothing compared with what poor old Worzel G. has to stomach with his pack of Reds baying for blood and old Benn back on the rampage, bronzed and fit and mad as a hatter. I only discovered the true cause the other day. The man is a total abstainer. No chance of his notes, I fear, being found blowing about on the rubbish tips of Leicestershire. . .

Sorry to hear about the Major's prang. I'll try and visit him in hospital over the weekend.

Yours aye,
DENIS

10 Downing Street

Whitehall

11 SEPTEMBER 1981

Dear Bill,

As you will have seen from the Press, I made quite a little killing at the betting shop on the Massacre of the Wets. Old Cemetery Face Gilmour was given short shrift, likewise Fatty S. and poor old Carlisle, who between you and me had been hitting it a bit of late — and who can blame him?

The Boss is cock-a-hoop about her points victory over Old Farmer Prior. I thought he was pushing his luck a bit, blabbing to the reptiles about what he would or would not do in the line of duty. On no account was he going to be driven into exile on the Bogside, rather resign and go back to growing mangel worzels. Sure enough there was one hell of a scrap at breakfast, and I saw Prior coming out red in the face and puffing, saying he'd never been so insulted in all his life, how had I managed it all these years, I must be a wreck, etc. He then asked if he could use the phone in Boris's office, and B. very kindly played it through to me on the tape afterwards. The party at the other end, as I soon realised, was our seafaring friend E. Heath, speaking from a Gym & Health Sauna somewhere in Marylebone. The Farmer started off in a mood of high dudgeon, and lost no time in reviling the Boss. This obviously music to E. Heath's ears, "splendid, splendid", Pinko P. could sit next to him on the back benches, they could have regular health food lunches to coordinate their plans, orchestrate opposition etc. At this I detected a slight cooling in Prior's rebellious tone. Heath presses on: Prior must realise of course that as the Senior Dissident, he Heath will of course take the chair at any discussions, but Prior could obviously come in under Stevarse, what fun, Norman so amusing, etc. What about dinner tonight, the three of them, to celebrate? The sound of backtracking now became deafening, Farmer P. began to mutter about no definite conclusion, offer of Northern Ireland job real challenge to patriotic duty, difficult task, Willie Whitelaw playing up historical perspective, and sure enough, later that day the Boss came in with a mad gleam in her eye to announce that Jim had seen the light and was even now buckling on his bullet-proof underwear en route for Belfast. But, as I may have said before, if a man can't stand up to Len Murray, what hope in hell has he when confronted with that mad bugger Paisley?

A propos the Workers by Hand and Brain, M. has now wheeled out some snotty little ex-airline pilot called Tebbit to wield the big stick. He started off well enough, telling all and sundry to bloody well pull their socks up and work harder. Needless to say, some wag pointed out that if they hadn't got any work in the first place how the hell could they do it any harder? Personally I thought that was a bit cheap, and anyway, when a new chap comes in, albeit up through the ranks, you should give him a moment or two to collect himself before pulling his trousers down.

My main concern at present, as you may have gathered from the media, is extricating myself from a very tricky situation with the Boss. Do you remember that friend of Maurice's who had a scheme to build pre-fab housing estates in the Lake District? Monty Greenstone, I think his name was, rather a shifty little cove with vicuna coat and sideburns. A few months back now, he and Maurice took me out to lunch at the RAC. Would I be consultant in exchange for a generous consignment of firewater — nothing through the books, obviously — to a little construction firm they were starting up to develop the National Parks? Here was all this land, going to rack and ruin, nothing but a handful of sheep, what better than a few motels, fast food shops, chalet-style executive second homes to liven things up a bit?

After a goodly number of scoops and stickies, the prospect began to look very rosy, whereupon the Greenstone bird stroked his moustache a bit, and said there was a minor snag. Planning wallahs dragging their heels over the Snowdonia Leisure Complex, Welsh Nat yobboes playing silly buggers, while shareholders' capital unfruitfully tied up. Next thing I knew G and P were back at No 10, making inroads into Boris's secret cache of pre-Revolutionary Vodka, and hammering something out on the Olivetti to which Yours Truly was duly required to append his monicker. I have no clear recollection of what it was, but something or other to the Minister responsible telling him to give the Planning Mob a boot up the arse, pull their fingers out and get weaving.

Naturally I thought no more about it at the time: Greenstone bloke stuffed it away in his crocodile combination-lock briefcase, more camaraderie and embracing and the two of them drove off in their Porsche, watched with a knowing eye by the Constable on duty.

Now some mischief-maker has burgled the file, fed the letter to the reptiles, and I am once again well and truly in the doghouse. Declaration of all my business interests to be handed in to Boss's study by 8am, plus a signed assurance that in future official stationery will not be used by my friends or acquaintances to promote their dubious enterprises: this all accompanied by invidious comparisons to Wilson's secretary woman and her slagheaps. So I advise you, for a start, when you've finished reading this to put it to the usual use.

Yours up to here,
DENIS

THE DON BRADMAN
INTERNATIONAL HOTEL
ADELAIDE ROAD
MELBOURNE

9 OCTOBER 1981

Dear Bill,
I don't know if you've ever been Down Under, but it's a bit like Esher used to be before the war. Nothing much happens, but a goodly number of snorts disappear down the hatch every night and the bar stays open till breakfast time. Of course, being the other side of the world geographically everything's the wrong way round, so that we're awake when you're asleep, and I think it's spring here, rather than whatever's going on up

your end. A cove I met in the little bar last night even told me that the bath-water goes out back to front and we both went up to M's bathroom to experiment. Unfortunately, when we got there, neither of us could remember which way it went out in England. M. came in in her curlers and that put a stop to our researches pretty pronto.

As you've probably read in the *Telegraph*, we're all fore-gathered for the Commonwealth Conference. Personally I thought the whole business had been wound up years ago, but not a bit of it. All the Coons, the Gandhi woman, little fellows who've obviously never had a suit on in their lives from places you only hear about if you collect stamps: there's nothing they like more, it seems, than having a week-long get-together to talk about the old days, just like the Major with his Service Corps chums booking that hotel every year in Taunton and getting blotto for days on end.

I was on parade at the opening shindig when they all sat down in a semi-circle with their flags for the Group Photo, one of those camera contraptions that goes round in a circle worked by clockwork, and the chairman, an Indian johnny, had hardly burbled his way through his speech of welcome when, blow me, up pops one of the Coons and begins berating little Muldoon from New Zealand for letting the Springboks do their Tour. Coons all Hear-Hearing away like a pack of monkeys, which really got my goat, Bill, I don't mind telling you. It was on the tip of my tongue to just ask them straight out what right they had to pick on a few inoffensive Kiwis punting the oval ball about with Friend Boer when there were literally millions upon millions of innocent people working in the salt mines of Siberia for cocking a snook at old Brezhnev. However, I caught the glint in M's eye and held my peace.

After that we were all invited aboard HM's floating gin palace, which she very sensibly had taken the precaution of mooring just off the point, well supplied with all fifty-seven varieties of plonk. At this, things did loosen up for a bit, and the Duke and I managed to lug Muldoon out of it for a while for iced tinctures in the B-Deck Saloon. It turned out we had a mutual friend in Arblaster, who used to ref for a while in the West Country, and apparently has now gone very badly to seed in Singapore.

Like me, Muldoon couldn't quite make out what the whole caper was in aid of, but the Duke explained that it went back to Queen Victoria. He himself had suggested over and over again that they should wind the whole thing up, particularly after we'd joined the Euro Business and weren't buying any more New Zealand Mutton Chops. But the Coons wouldn't hear of it, and nor would his Missus. The talk was obviously all piss and wind, but HM got a real kick out of sitting on the throne while the Paramount Chiefs kissed her feet and gave her monkeyskin handbags and ivory toothpicks, particularly that little Nyerere. These feelings were entirely reciprocated by the Fuzzy-wuzzies, even those who are hand in glove with Moscow and Peking. The Duke's a very wise old bean, and his theory is that his better half is regarded as some kind of Ju Ju object. You've got to remember, he says, that most of these chaps are tribal chiefs at heart, even though they wear shiny shoes and read books by Lenin.

I learnt from my airmail copy of the *Telegraph* that you are all getting steamed up again about Interest Rates, Howe taking a lot of stick on the mortgage front, CBI wallahs foaming at the mouth, M. bankrupting the country etc. All I can say is that from down here, by the pool, where I have spent the remainder of this balls-aching cavalcade, it all seems a very very long way away. However, I did notice in the small print that the Natwest deposit rate has shot up again very satisfactorily, which, even taking the taxman into account, must be good news for all of us. As I told the Boss at a beach barbecue we had to attend with the tall cove who at present lords it over the convict hordes, it's only the ne'erdowells like Maurice P. who run up debts at the bank who have anything to complain about. The Wise Virgins, like you and me and the Major, with our little nest-eggs, are very much in the old girl's debt and must support her policies up to the hilt. And what ever old Worzel may have said in Brighton, little Benn seems to be doing a splendid job.

Talking of Maurice, I did my best to help during our mercifully brief stopover at Bahrain Airport. I was meant to pass on a parcel of lagging material with a view to shifting some of his surplus from the warehouse at Deal onto the unsuspecting Sons of the Desert. Alas, my contact had been arrested only moments before, and I was just in time to see him being bundled unceremoniously into a waiting paddywagon.

Any chance of your joining me to spread the load of misery at Blackpool?

Yours in hope,

DENIS

Dear Bill,

I don't know whether you've ever been to Blackpool — I have a dim inkling we discussed this before — but it really is the most ghastly dump. I can't understand why they choose it. It takes absolutely hours to get to from anywhere, then when you finally make it there's nothing but mile upon mile of Bingo Saloons, Space Invaders, sticky rock shops and Chinese Takeaways, and the plebs from Manchester and the Potteries gawping about on the Prom, all too ready to poke fun at their betters.

This year, Saatchis had booked us into the Barcelona Country Club, right out in the sticks, formerly the seat of some local mill-owner, and now run by a Mr and Mrs Len Wallop with a taste for piped music, plastic flowers, tropical fish let into the wall, and a few back numbers of *Lancashire Country Life* scattered about like they are at the dentist's. The snag, as I discovered on footing it downstairs for a recce on arrival, was the Health Juice Bar. Mr Len, it transpired, after hitting it fairly heavily out East, had come within a whisker of extinction in 1953 and signed the Pledge. Mrs Len verified this story with copious anecdotes of how much better he felt, and would you think he was only 76?

As good fortune would have it, I collided in an upper corridor with our Home Secretary, looking very down in the mouth about this state of affairs, and ere long a Special Branch van had backed up to his window, and helmeted officers were ferrying in assorted crates for discreet storage behind the sofa in Whitelaw's sitting room. Thus we were both able to fortify ourselves after breakfast each morning for the long ordeal beneath the burning lights.

The smell in the conference room was as usual unspeakable, and I was issued with the standard Order of the Day by the Boss, i.e. no clapping for the Wets, stay awake at all times, avoid nose picking, yawning, unseemly laughter, overt displays of boredom, etc.

All eyes, needless to say, were on old Sailorboy Ted when he bustled up to hold forth on the second day. The Press reptiles, as you may have seen, had worked up a phoney crisis with a lot of excitable talk about Teddy Benn and the Big Split, Boss at any moment about to be toppled, back-bench rumblings and all the usual palaver. Fortunately you've only got to take one look at Heath to realise he couldn't topple a blancmange off a plate. He always reminds me of that old bachelor party who used to run the Company Flat for Burmah in Ennismore Gardens. You remember we all used to speculate about what he got up to in his spare time with no definite proof of his proclivities being furnished, even by Harris the company driver. You used to sneer at me for saying this, but it was always my opinion that he was one of life's non-combatants, who are, if truth be told, thicker on the ground than a perusal of Page Three of the *Daily Telegraph* would lead you to believe. The same, I suspect, is true of our Lost Leader.

As soon as he stepped up on the podium and little Parkinson banged down the egg-timer, I could see from my vantage point that the troops were preparing themselves for twenty minutes under the parapet. A few brave souls weathered the flood of boredom to shout this and that, but even they were ground down by the Yachtsman's remorseless recitative. Three people, presumably former cabin crew aboard the Morning Cloud, rose to their feet at the conclusion to try and prise the assembled burghers off their arses, but if ever there was a lost cause, Bill, that was it. I was put painfully in mind of the time the Major got the bird, essaying his George Formby impersonation at the Rotary Outing to Wendover.

Not a difficult act to follow, you might think, Bill, and you would be right. Little Howe, glasses gleaming and fresh from the hairdressers, got a few good laughs from reading out some gems of early Heath, excavated from the archives by one of his eager beavers at the Treasury — "No Going Back", "Inflation Top Priority", "Must Pay Our Way", i.e. all the same old balls the Boss has been trotting out ever since she emerged at the top of the heap. In brief. E. Heath hoist with his own whatever it is you get hoisted with.

After that, lesser fry like Cemetery Face and Stevarse were mere cats' meat. However I did tell the Boss to keep a wary eye on Tarzan. Ever since he went off on his famous slum-crawl in Liverpool, pressing the flesh with all those discontented coons and street corner skinheads who've never done a day's work in their lives and wouldn't recognise a job if they saw one, I have had the clear impression that our Ginger has been looking for an opening to come in on the inside and pip M. to the post in the final furlong, hence his extensive bet-hedging and bleating on about One Nation, which is pretty ripe coming from him.

You've probably seen that the work-shy yobboes at BL are once again up to their seasonal pranks. I told the Boss that now surely we can come out of the closet and close the whole thing down once and for all. Here we are, allegedly in power and pledged to strangle every lame duck in sight, and we are pumping a million pounds a minute into the Longbridge Christmas piss-up fund, all to no avail. For good measure I passed on to M. the sad story of Maurice Picarda's Metro. According to his lady-friend it ground to a halt in the fast lane of the M1 just North of the Watford Gap, and when he finally got a breakdown truck out from Hemel Hempstead, all four wheels fell off, the gear lever came away in his hand, and when he got out to show it to the mechanic the whole thing blew up and caught fire. Typically of Maurice, he had failed to take out any insurance but I didn't tell the Boss that bit.

Any chance of a day trip down to Huntercombe before the clocks go back? I bought some new togs in Australia and I am quite keen to try them out in the bar.

Yours in perpetuity,

DENIS

10 Downing Street
Whitehall
6 NOVEMBER 1981

Dear Bill,

Thank you on your condolences on my being dropped from the squad for the Autumn Summit Break to Mexico but, quite honestly, after being left standing about all over Australia I was very glad to have a few days on my ownsome. I'd been meaning to have a blitz on the Den for months. Boris has been helping me to clear out the empties that have been gathering dust under the bed and behind the Wisdens, and I made a parcel of old clothes and broken golf clubs for Mrs Prosser's Jumble down in Kent in aid of her brain-damaged jockeys, in which I included various bribes and mementoes that Maurice had sent me from time to time, like that ghastly platinum desk lamp made in the shape of three ladies eating a lollipop, for which Mrs P. seemed duly grateful.

I understand the Mexican jaunt was the usual hell on wheels, though the Boss obviously enjoyed herself no end. Plenty of hot air both inside and outside the chamber, old Hopalong flying in to deliver his thoughts on helping the Third World, or the South as it is now called — the kind of thing Heath's always banging away about. M. and Carrington made a bravish stab at telling the assembled Coons and Commies to pull their socks up, but from what I gathered the message was considerably watered down from my original draft. As you know, I was out East only this year, being wined and dined by the Gandhi woman, and you don't need to look much beyond the airport perimeter to realise that the natives in those parts have no desire whatsoever to get off their arses and go to the office —let alone the lavatory, from the state of the streets. A lot of them are so bone idle they prefer to lie down and die on the pavement rather than make the effort of clocking in at the Labour Exchange. So what on earth — and this was my spiel to little Carrington before he left — is the point of people like Maurice going out there and trying to get them interested in making double-glazing units? As to the Africans, you remember Wilkinson's experience trying to build that flyover in Khartoum. And how can we be expected to shell out millions of pounds to the sun-tanned ragamuffins

when we're rapidly disappearing down the drain ourselves passes my imagination. But it's no good expecting sense from politicos like Carrington. They like going off on these freebies and confabs in sunny climes just to get away from it all.

You have to hand it to the Boss, she flew back cool as a cucumber, despite earthquakes and the foreign food, eager to climb into the ring for a vicious ten rounds with poor old Worzel, who once again got whirled about, lost his specs, had his head thumped on the floor and a couple of fingers up his nostrils from Brer Enoch for good measure. Even Margaret's Wets raised a feeble cheer as the Old Philosopher's dentures hit the light, but despite the general glee they're all, if you ask me, pretty windy about the Alliance people, who put up some hopeless little runt with a beard in Croydon North West and swept the board. Now the woman with the untidy hair who gets Margaret's goat is off giant-killing in Manchester, planning to demolish a 19,000 Tory majority before breakfast, and the thought of any female competition in the Talking Shop is obviously fraying the proprietorial nerves more than somewhat, though my view, which I have often expressed to the Boss, is that until she can come to grips with her hair she can't be treated as a serious political threat.

I am glad to see that BL seems bent on the Kamikaze-style exit. That awful little South African creep Edwardes is obviously packing his rat-like luggage prior to disembarking from the doomed vessel, and I imagine the Japs will be swarming in to take over ere long. Shades of Singapore all over again, what, Bill? Some of us at least may get a chuckle or two out of seeing those workshy yobboes at Longbridge being thrashed about by the Nip guards as they slave over the Changi assembly lines on their daily half a bowl of rice. Would you believe it? Maurice, like a damn fool, has ordered their new Acclaim. Quite apart from his previous experience with the exploding Metro, I told him he'd be damned lucky to see it before next summer, or indeed at all, the way things are going. Thank heaven I've still got the Rolls is all I can say. I think she'll probably see me out, if I can prevent that bugger Mark from getting his evil little hands on it.

Yours in the rough,

DENIS

Dear Bill,

I sometimes think Margaret leads a charmed life. Did you see old Worzel on the Church Parade at the Cenotaph? I was stationed in a rear rank with some minor royalty, coons' wives, British Legion Cadet Corps etc and a few miscellaneous body-guards, but I still got a pretty good view of events up front. I'm not usually one to shed a manly tear at these capers, but having fortified myself against the cold with a stiff sharpener or twain before setting out, I found the effect of the brass band and the long greatcoats very moving, and couldn't help thinking of old chums like Tuppy Hornblower who bought it during the last lot. (I know he had a stroke playing silly buggers in the Mess at a Guest Night with the RASC but in my book that counts as Active Service if anything does.)

Picture the scene, Bill. Sun streaming down Whitehall, a few last brown leaves scratching along the pavement, assembled Royalty, M., little Steel etc all standing rigidly to attention, the note of the bugle dies away, the great bell tolls and a solemn silence falls over the Heart of the Empire. At moments like this you feel that everything is not in vain. Then, blow me — Worzel, who has already attracted a good many black looks from the Royal Box by turning up in a silly tie and some kind of German donkey jacket out of a Millet's sale, begins to fidget, pick his nose and scratch his arse as if waiting for the Number 11 bus. When it comes to the wreath-laying he shambles up in his brothel creepers and plonks it down like a poor old codger putting the empties out and totters back to resume his monkeyhouse act at the Proprietor's shoulder. As if this wasn't enough, he then keeps his mouth firmly shut during "Oh God Our Help In Ages Past" on the grounds that he's a paid-up non-believer and professional God-botherer, and doesn't believe a word of it. Not that that stops him singing the Red Flag in Blackpool. I could see the D of E going purple in the face, and all the Top Brass looked to be building up for a visit to the cardiac unit.

I expected Margaret, when we got indoors, would be fit to be tied, but not a bit of it. Old girl cock-a-hoop, large stickies

all round. Peter Carrington being stuffy about it — Worzel had
failed his medical for the '39 show, frightful little pen-pusher
etc — but Boss cuts him short, pointing out the whole thing has
been on the telly, Worzel must have been losing votes like air
out of a burst tyre. I couldn't help feeling a bit sorry for poor
old Foot all the same. I was reminded of the time that fellow
Ginger Withers turned up at the Burmah Christmas Lunch
wearing a dinner jacket when it said Informal on the card and
we all threw bread rolls at him just to drive the point home.
Personally I blame the wife in Worzel's case. She put him up
for the job in the first place, and she should see to it that he is
properly accoutred for all occasions and knows where he's
meant to be going, like the Boss does with yours truly.

How long he can stand it in the hot seat I really can't imagine. They were all hoping that after the Blackpool show-down the Mad Tea-Drinker Benn, he of the permanently revolving eyes, would now come to heel. Not a bit of it. Last week apparently there was some debate down at the Talking Shop about North Sea Gas, the official Labour Rep spools out the Party Line, up pops Benn like a Jack-in-the-Box, quivering with excitement, foam flecking his lips, and announces that when he comes to power the whole of the North Sea will be sequestered, not a penny compensation paid to the shareholders, and all foreign oil men publicly strung up by the thumbs in Parliament Square. Worzel blows fuse and is assisted from Chamber.

So long as this goes on, Saatchi's view is that M. is as safe as houses, though there is the snag of the SDP. You know my views about the Woman with the Hair, but I do rather take my hat off to the Owen cove. Did you see him trying to strangle that Student yobbo at Sussex University? Some awful little Trot slinging rotten vegetables at him and clearly something snapped. Not that I have any sympathy with Owen personally, who is clearly some kind of smarmy, jumped-up Houseman, but it was high time someone struck a blow at all those work-shy monkeys sponging off their Student Grants and smoking dope all day at our expense when they could be working on the roads. A propos, you see that little wooftah Livingstone has had his balls given a pretty good tweak in the High Court by old Gaffer Denning. That'll teach him to try and bring down the Tube Fares. So all in all things are going our way, I'd say.

Do you fancy the enclosed freebie weekend in Bloemfontein? Booze all the way, some kind of casino being opened by the Major's Battle of Britain chum who got nicked for the VAT fiddle, and I'm told a very good little course.

Yours in hope,

DENIS

Dear Bill,

I don't know whether it's percolated to your neck of the woods, but the Boss's lot took a terrible hammering up on Merseyside. The tousle-haired temptress swept in like a white tornado, the only comfort being that Worzel's man lost his deposit. I can't understand what they see in the Williams woman, not to mention that smarmy little GP or the fat cat from Brussels with the speech impediment. If ever there was a set of hopeless hand-job merchants those are they.

And yet perfectly sane human beings appear to have fallen under their spell. Harken to what follows. On the Night of the Crosby Long Knives, scenting the wrath to come — the Boss sitting up late in front of three television sets, valium jar at her elbow — I thought it prudent to make myself scarceish, and accepted a phone invite from Maurice to join him and a few friends whooping it up in an American's flat in Paddington.

I arrived, self-driven, to find our old friend wearing a shiny new suit, dispensing largish snorts to a motley gang of hangers-on, the usual car-salesmen, laundromat proprietors and their ladies, all quite jolly, and Maurice, I observed with relief, noticeably abstemious, apparently being taken in hand by a large divorcee from the Personnel Department at the Army & Navy Stores.

Our American host did not seem to be present, slosh was available in ample doses, and the Personnel lady weaving her way through the throng replenishing our glasses in a very understanding way. I found myself talking to a very amusing little woman who teaches Yoga at a health farm somewhere out near Tring, and we were getting on like a house on fire with her showing me the basic holds when Maurice suddenly took his shoe off and hammered on the sideboard to call us all to order. For one ghastly moment I thought he was going to announce his engagement like he did that time in Rye. Then I saw he had a wad of brightly coloured handouts, and naturally assumed we were all about to be given the Picwarmth Hard Sell and touched for a few thou apiece with the usual

spiel about twenty percent off to shareholders if we placed a firm order before Christmas.

Not a bit of it Bill. Would you believe our friend has seen the light? "The old two-party system has had its day, a time to break the mould, no Tory seat ever safe again, only hope for small businesses, generous grants, firm belief in profitability, we all need reflating, M. Picarda hoping to stand for Sevenoaks in the SDP interest." Well, Bill, you could have knocked me down with a barn door, especially as by this stage I was not altogether steady on my feet. A moment later various television screens leapt to life, Mrs Crosby was seen bindling about looking cheery, and in due course, in the small hours, the Lord Mayor or whoever he was read out the score to wild cheering, at which point Maurice's seedy friends went absolutely bananas, some kind of supermarket fizzy drink was produced, and Maurice made another speech, somewhat less coherent than the first.

Having had my arm twisted for a fat contribution to party funds, I was not in the best of moods as I piloted the Rolls back to the sanctuary of Downing Street, only to find some joker had plastered the roof with damnfool stickers for the SDP. As I tiptoed up the wooden hill I could hear the Boss picking over the pieces with poor old Whitelaw, who was looking very flushed and weepy and had obviously given up the idea of staying sober.

If you ask me, this all bodes v. ill for the Boss, and U-Turns are clearly not being excluded from the scenario. They've all been in the Talking Shop trying to cobble something up in the way of a sop, without, I may say, much success. The latest news is that any minute now Brother Howe will shuffle into the Lion's Den and announce yet another dose of salts by way of Christmas Cheer, i.e. higher TV licences, more on false teeth and glasses, cuts in the dole and a short sharp shock for the long-haired student yobboes and their bank managers. This last absolutely makes sense to me, though needless to say the smart arses up and down Whitehall will continue to live out the evenings of their idle lives on generous index-linked pensions, e.g. that friend of Daph's sister at Esher, Sir Whatsisname, the one who dresses up in women's clothes.

This latest package has been cooked up by two of Margaret's new backroom boys, a shifty little lawyer called

Brittain and his smarmy little sidekick with bouffant hair name of Lawson, a former reptile, chiefly notorious a few years back for landing a whopping mortgage. A couple of sharks, if you ask me, very reminiscent of those two street Arabs who used to cook the books for Maurice when he was running his Afternoon Drinking Club in Hendon. As for Friend Tebbit, the less said the better. The idea that our Norman would strike fear into the hearts of Len Murray and the Smelly Socks Brigade is quite laughable, and what our lot says about him behind his back doesn't bear repeating.

By the by, not a word to a soul, but the only pleasure the Boss has had all week was over poor old Fatty Prior getting roughed up at the Funeral by the Animal Paisley and his Heavy Mob. A propos, have you spotted the odd-looking fuzzy-haired Gyppo figure who trails along in Prior's wake, grinning like a golliwog? The Major's theory is that he is some sort of poet on the run from the House of Lords, but I can't believe even Margaret would be as foolish as that. Still, it's a rum old world.

Could you do your usual re the Yuletide Hooch from the Cash 'n' Carry? On four crates the saving is really quite dramatic.

Yours in anticipation,
DENIS

10 Downing Street
Whitehall

18 DECEMBER 1981

Dear Bill,

I don't know whether the Major has rung you with the news of his Scott of the Antarctic expedition last week. We'd arranged to meet at the Club at ten for pre-lunch snorts, and at five past twelve he staggered in, snow on his boots and badly frost-bitten. It was only after four large brownies that he felt minded to unfold his tale.

Apparently he had left Eastbourne, where he had been staying with Mrs Frobisher, on the seven-fifteen, and just after East Croydon they ground to a halt in drifts some half an inch deep, known to British Rail as Adverse Weather Conditions.

An hour later they were still there, windows steaming up, tempers v. frayed, no one around to say what was going on, the Pakistani Conductor having locked himself in the lavatory for fear of reprisals. Fortunately the Major had a bottle in his overnight bag and, finally, emboldened by a stiffish swig or twain, he decided to climb down on the line and walk, accompanied by a couple of other stalwarts from BP.

It appears they had miscalculated somewhat in imagining they were just outside Victoria, and after an hour's steady trudge over the snow-covered sleepers, they met a man from the Railways who said they had paralysed the entire system. At this the Major saw red, and the old boy has now got to present himself before the beak at Wandsworth sometime in the new year.

He asked me if I could put in a word with Sir Peter Parker, but after what happened last time I put in a word on behalf of an old friend I am somewhat chary of repeating the experience. Anyway I told him that Parker was far too busy whizzing up and down on his Flying Banana from London to Glasgow with charred toasted sandwiches flying about his ears and perfectly good plonk going to waste by the crateload, smashed to smithereens every time they go round a bend.

Meanwhile, pre-Christmas Tension is building up nicely, and I took the liberty of suggesting it might be the main plank in the Major's defence when he comes to Court. M. has a miniature rebellion on her hands, with Cemetery Face and his little band of Wets frothing at the mouth about the dole money being cut, when it seems to me to be the most sensible thing they've done for a long time. Here we have, Bill, three million or so workshy yobboes sitting at home watching The Two Ronnies, cigars and tawny port to hand at the expense of hardworking chaps like you and me, what better than a blast of cold air, a short sharp shock from Brother Howe to get them up off their arses and bindling about looking for odd jobs like mowing the Major's lawn? But Old Cemetery Face lives in a world of his own, quite out of touch with ordinary people. Ditto our Sailorboy friend, who has also been huffing and puffing, keeping a weather eye open for any bandwagon he can conceivably clamber on that will restore him to supreme power.

Also getting stick, I am pleased to say, is that ghastly streak of piss David Howell, who has deemed it politic to throw open our country lanes to bigger and better juggernauts, thereby incurring the wrath of the Home Counties Brigade, who find it impossible to close an eye in their thatched Tudor mansions for fear some metal-encased fragment of the butter mountain should remove the granny annexe. You remember what happened that night poor old Podmore bought it while painting a message of good cheer outside his Uckfield love nest!

Worzel's travails, as you may have surmised from a cursory view of the *Daily Telegraph*, are also still far from over. Fresh from falling down an organ shaft en route to address the faithful, he decided to wreak vengeance on a cruel world by lashing out at some innocent little Australian Gayboy whose only offence was that he had been selected to stand in the Labour interest for some bombsite or other south of the Thames. Predictably, every Trot in creation has come crawling out of his Moscow-subsidised rat-hole baying for blood, Benn has shed his straitjacket and returned to the fray, eyes ablaze and threatening to fight like a tomcat in the cause of free speech for all. Naturally the Boss is laying down Port in consequence, and has taken to doing press-ups in Hyde Park in preparation for the next twenty years in office.

On a gloomier front, I must decline your kind invite for Boxing Day snorts, as we shall be doing the usual Chequers routine, fledgelings returning to the nest, etc. Mark is proposing this year to delight us with his latest flame, a busty divorcee from Yorkshire who runs a home-made jewellery outfit somewhere near Kettering, you know the type, sheepskin and a Jag and too much lipstick. I anticipate that the central heating will be on the blink as per usual, and we are experimenting this year with a Bolivian couple recommended by the Carringtons. All in all a melancholy vista, I think you will agree.

Forgive the Christmas Card. It's meant to be M. and self in August at the Saatchis' behest, hence my somewhat roseate features.

Yours six feet under,

DENIS

Chequers

1 JANUARY 1982

Dear Bill,

Should this ever reach you, very best wishes to you and Daphne for 1982. The only good news is that your very thoughtful crates from the Cash and Carry got through before the big freeze up. I agree with you about the Glen Fiji Triple Strength. When I downed my first gulp I thought the top of my head would come off. Pow! After the sixth or seventh one got the hang of it. But God, Bill, has it been needed!

Margaret had the damnfool idea that she would bring the car down and work off a bit of her aggression on the M.40. The little weather bloke with the moustache forecasted a mild night with a slow thaw heading in from the West turning to warm rain on high ground. Boris bundled the prezzies, turkey, crackers and various seasonal freebies from British Industry, the Wog Embassies etc into the boot of the Rolls, I climbed into the passenger seat well swathed in rugs and hip flask at the ready, and away we purred.

We hit our first minor snag just north of Paddington, where a juggernaut had jack-knifed across the flyover and there was a tailback of some one and a half miles. Snow was falling heavily, A.A. on the radio advising everyone to stay at home, coon teenagers strolling up and down the jam thumping on the roof and shouting abuse. Consolation from the Boss to the effect that things are much worse than this in Poland. Boris says no. According to him, Solidarity blowing up the coalmines, Trots and agitators teeming under every bed, Walesa the worst type of Scargill figure, this General Jabberwocky only doing his patriotic duty, all in all valuable object lesson for the Boss and she should be on her guard for a coup probably led by Mad Mike Hoare at the end of January.

As so often with Boris, I couldn't help feeling there might be a grain of truth in his analysis. I was talking to Furniss at the NatWest over a pre-Christmas snorto de luxe, and he tells me that they've been lending the Polaks bloody billions over the last few years, all on the assumption that if the solids hit the fan, brother Russky would toddle in and foot the bill. Not so. Deep gloom at head office. Only hope now for getting their pound of flesh pinned on the good General and his dynamic style of leadership. I told Furniss I didn't think it would work for a moment, knowing the workers, but when you think Bill, that our hard-earned deposits are being poured down some bottomless hole in the ground in Silesia it really makes you wonder what it's all about.

A propos, should I ever get out of here alive, I wouldn't mind lunch with your broker friend at some stage to talk about growth prospects. The Boss suggests in a high handed way I ought to put it all into National Savings Geriatric Bonds, the Government being so desperate for cash they're offering 15% tax free. But having seen Howe and Co at close quarters I don't really warm to the idea of trusting them with anything like money.

Meanwhile, inch by inch, we headed into Darkest Bucks, hypothermia cases stumbling about in the snow flailing their arms, verges laden with abandoned cars, and arrived at Chequers at 4.30a.m. to find that Mr Wu, while loyally trying to clear the drive, had fallen over once again and been taken to Stoke Mandeville. The promised Indonesian couple engineered by the Carringtons had apparently had a flaming row with their last employers in Hampstead and were now in custody pending extradition. This left Yours Truly to act as Major Domo, cum Head Cook and Bottlewasher over the festive tide.

Before doing anything I decided that a sharpener would not come amiss. However, when I spun the kitchen tap to dilute the aforementioned Fiji, nothing came out. Margaret now in a huff retired to the freezing bedroom to bury herself under a mound of blankets, leaving me to polish off crate and discover the whereabouts of tank. I can't remember whether you've ever been down to our company accommodation here at Chequers but the upstairs part is an absolute rabbit-warren. Everything you expect to be a room is a cupboard and vice versa. Luckily Boris seemed to know his way about, and was able after a couple of hours to report that he had unfrozen the tank, and that one tap in the gun room was now producing rusty water. Raising our glasses to celebrate this little success, we were immediately plunged into terrible darkness.

I will pass over subsequent events Margaret having been in very high spirits throughout, insisting that it is all good practice for the Total War on the Miners, now billed as our New Year attraction. Boris left some hours ago a la Captain Oates, feeling he'd be less of a drain on the dwindling booze supplies. The only consolation is that the little perisher Mark didn't get through with his bit of stuff from Yorks. Tell the boys I went down bottle in hand.

Yours,

DENIS

10 Downing Street
Whitehall

15 JANUARY 1982

Dear Bill,

When are you off to Barbados, you lucky bugger? I do hope you manage to get away: you remember Batty Dugdale, one of the Burmah reps in the South West? I bumped into him in the Club the other morning, very much the worse for wear after three days at snowbound Luton with his Missus and the grandchildren, waiting for a package Jumbo to whip them off to South Africa and sanity, all to no avail. I never liked the look of that Laker chap. Has a lot to answer for, in my view, encouraging the great unwashed to take to the airways, thus buggering it up for the rest of us.

We are all sitting here on tenterhooks, waiting to see which way the Miners will jump. Unofficially, the word is not a penny more than nine per cent, M. prepared to fight to the last OAP etc, and the same for Mr Buckton's little band of Bolshies. (The effects of the rail strike are in any case irrelevant as the whole bang shoot has frozen up due to the lack of hot water bottles to lay over the points.) In fact, if you ask me, the Boss is all of a tremble, dreading a showdown with King Arthur. Last year, you may remember, they all caved in at the first squeak from Brother Gormley, who was furthermore quite a decent little NCO. This time, with the wild-eyed Red from Barnsley calling the tune, I have a feeling you won't see Margaret's arse for dust.

Personally I blame Carrington. As I think I told you on a previous occasion, Bill, he had something of a traumatic experience sharing the bridge with Skipper Heath during the dark hours of the three-day week, and whenever the word 'Miners' is mentioned the colour drains from his face and I have to do my St Bernard act with the Sticky Bottle. This doesn't stop him banging the drum over the Polacks. As you know, he and the Boss are convinced that the sun shines out of Old Hopalong's fundament, though personally I could never see it, and this Haig man who acts as gopher for the old cove is all for a shoot-out with Brother Russky to demonstrate who's top dog.

Carrington, therefore, has been buzzing about using all the old Etonian sap on greasing up to the Euros and trying to charm them into line for Hopalong's Mr Universe number. Old Schmidt, the snuff-taking Hun, is refusing to come to heel. Furniss, our little friend at the NatWest, explained it all to me over a schooner or so of his Amontillado in the manager's office the other morning. Schmidt and his banking friends have all got a lot of spondulicks tied up on the other side of the Iron Curtain, and their fervent hope is that this General Whatsisname will restore a bit of profitability to the whole undertaking and thus enable them to retrieve their fifteen per cent. I think I told you last time, even normally reasonable souls like the NatWest have been dabbling in these troubled waters, and it's all very well for old Hopalong to take a highminded line when his own investments are safely tucked away in South America.

We all had a good laugh at Worzel's Peace In Our Time stuff at the end of their Special Conference. Do you remember that episode in the history books where a poor dithering old king was bullied out to Runnymede to put his monicker to some kind of Bill of Rights by various burly Barons? Apparently much the same took place at Bishop Stortford: poor old Worzel dragged in in chains by the Union jackasses and told there would be no more cash until he and Benn kissed and made up in public. Everyone managed to keep a straight face, and the reptiles were dispatched to proclaim peace in banner headlines in all the Tory newspapers. Meanwhile, Saatchis appear to have been active in the ranks of the SDP. Maurice got a poison-pen letter, presumably emanating from their office, warning him to keep away from Sevenoaks or the Liberals would let his tyres down, but the old boy is still determined to stand, and has put himself forward as Shadow Spokesman for Market Gardening.

No chance now of the day out to Huntercombe with the Major and Sticky. Apparently they both came a cropper tobogganing down from the Clubhouse and Wilkinson is now laid up with his back.

Give my regards to Curly the Barman at the Noel Coward Rooms should you ever reach the Island in the Sun.

Yours in cold storage,
DENIS

10 Downing Street
Whitehall
29 JANUARY 1982

Dear Bill,

Thank you for your condolences on the safe return of the son and h from his Sahara car rally. Honestly, what a prize twerp! I washed my hands of the little blighter years ago, and when the Boss told me he was intending to drive across the desert with some fancy French bint he'd picked up in the pits, my response was that he could go to hell in a handcart for all I cared. Next thing I know, M. is hammering on my door at some unearthly hour to say she has just heard on the Jimmy Young Show that the little bugger has been missing for four days and what was I going to do about it? Answer, turn over and go back to sleep. Cue for maternal hysteria, call myself a man, etc, why yours truly always so pathetic in a crisis? Eventually I found my glasses and endeavoured to pour a bit of oil on the troubled H2O, arguing that a) a bad penny usually turns up in the end and b) that being inexperienced in these matters he had probably driven off on one of the B-roads in search of a quiet layby to try a bit of hanky-panky with la belle frog. Need I tell you that this last analysis went down like a cup of cold sick, waterworks turned on, hanky out, male sex maligned, wailing and gnashing of teeth, all culminating in yours truly agreeing to jump on the first Laker standby to Timbuctoo in search of Prodigal Son.

Later: Proprietor now back on course, heading for show-down with the CBI, DT hurtles down to Gatwick, soon steadying the nerves with a largish brownie at thirty thousand feet, rudely jostled by reptiles, all treating the whole thing like a day trip to Boulogne, air blue with smutty anecdotes.

Touch down desert airstrip, local time 11.30p.m., a real dump if ever I saw one called Tamanrasset. (I had a dim memory that poor old Podmore bought it somewhere near there while serving with the Rats, but no matter.) Usual wog nonsense about no snorts, some smarmy little FO cove whispering out of the corner of his mouth about special arrangements at the Tam Hilton, and off we drive. Reptiles have beat us to it, and are soon drinking the place dry. Would you believe it, ten quid for a single? Obviously mine Host, Ali Baba, had seen them coming, and was asking a hundred quid a go for his Telex. It turned out that no one had the faintest clue the so-called race was even on. It had all been organised, if that is the word, out of a little office in Paris by a bunch of cowboys as a publicity stunt. In these times of high unemployment however an army of motorcycles, delivery vans, articulated trucks and every conceivable type of wheeled vehicle had set off from Marseilles to pit their wits against the hostile environment while the vultures circled overhead, scenting a bit of free grub.

Given such a bunch of hopeless layabouts at the wheel Mark was not the only one to have come to grief along the way, and in the meantime, thanks to the Boss hoisting storm cones, the entire Algerian airforce in the shape of three helicopters and an old Hercules was grinding through the sky overhead, in constant danger of collision with the squadron of French Mirages put up by Mitterand who seems to have taken a strange shine to the Boss. (Very decent of him, en passant, considering the man's a raving Red who has, you may remember, several times tried to arrest the NatWest's representative in Paris for issuing private chequebooks.)

I was sitting comfortably enough ensconced in the Lounge enjoying the patronage of the *Daily Telegraph* Motoring Correspondent when one of these pilot johnnies breezed in for a quick one and said would I like to go aloft in his kite for a shuftie at the terrain? Moments later we were bucketing about in the inky blackness, friend wog shouting back incomprehensible references to flickering lights beneath, and it crossed my mind that given a fair wind the Boss might soon have to send out another search party to bring in yours truly.

When we eventually returned, empty-handed, to the Bar, bugger me if young Mark isn't sitting there with a carefully nurtured growth of beard, drawling away to the reptiles, affecting great unconcern about the whole episode, and clearly seeing himself as the hero of the hour. At the first possible juncture I took the blighter to one side and gave him a pretty largish piece of my mind. Did he realise that the air forces of the entire Free World had been out trying to find him and his bit of French fluff for the last seventy two hours? That his mother was on the very brink of a breakdown? That I myself had had to come out to this Godforsaken oasis and would no doubt shortly be expected to partake of sheepseyes with the wog powers that be, and all because he refused to take a job like any other young man of his wealth and background? Absolutely no response. Sulky look, not his fault if parental brigade overreacts, he and Mamselle Fifi perfectly happy sitting in the desert waiting for the local A.A. man to turn up.

The rest, I imagine, is history. Flash-bulbs popping all the way back to Chequers. Unquestionably the worst moment of the whole episode, when Saatchis had invited every reptile in the business down for a photo call on the lawn, and it was suggested I should put my arm round the little sniveller as a sign of delirious happiness at the reunion. I drew the line at this despite a withering look from M., and broke away at the earliest moment to recover my equilibrium in the Waggonload of Monkeys.

The only other excitement, as you may have seen, was the Boss having to turf out Fairburn, the little bald lawyer in the kilt who got into all that hot water with a woman before Christmas. Fellow looked like a prize jackass to me, and I can't think why he ever got the job in the first place. I can only presume that all lawyers are randy, like that QC fellow who handled Maurice's divorce and tried to get off with ex Mrs P. some weeks later. I suppose it must be having all that money and nothing to do.

How would you feel about two days in the Seychelles at the beginning of February? I met a little man in the Club the other day called Davis who said he could fix it up.

Yours in anticipation,

DENIS

10 Downing Street
Whitehall
12 FEBRUARY 1982

Dear Bill,

What about this train strike, eh? Thank God for Mr Buckton and his merry band of Reds say I. As you've probably gathered from the shower of PCs flooding through your letterbox, Maurice P., the Major and I have been having a whale of a time at the Club. Of course the Major could perfectly well have driven up and down in his new Merc, but he told the wife that it was out of the question and he would have to stay three nights in town. I offered to put him up here but the Boss put her foot down, recalling previous occasions, smashed china, nocturnal singing, burned carpets etc. Maurice P. was on to some ' similar wheeze to get away from his Antique Hypermarket Woman, and spun a yarn about a three day SDP conference, which apparently she swallowed h, l and s. So they took a double room in the Ladies' Annexe.

I went round there on Wednesday night for a snort and there was a very good crowd assembled in the Snooker Room. Do you remember the log-burner chap from Wokingham we met on the boat? He was there, scattering twenty pound notes in all directions. Also a very entertaining little man with a squint, called Redhead, who organises cheapies from Luton Airport and said the next time we went to Portugal together he could certainly oblige with fifteen days all in for £87.25. Amazing when you come to think that the single in the same direction is twice that.

About nine-ish, things were getting fairly unbuttoned, Maurice P. offering his Russian Dance on the snooker table and the Redhead cove suggested a foray into Soho to a little downstairs joint for an entertainment entitled Paul Raymond's Festival of Uncensored Pagan Sin. Off we went. Usual racket about Life Membership, obligatory bottle of flat champagne for fifty quid, familiar depressing line up of clap cases jerking about in jackboots. Redhead, by now molto paralytico, began to shout various suggestions from the stalls and we were asked to leave by a pair of blue-chinned bruisers with Italian accents. All good fun, I think you'll agree, and as long as Parker stands firm I think we can bank on a repeat next week. Perhaps you might join us.

Back at Bleak House little Pym has blotted his copybook with all and sundry. I read the gist of what he had said in the evening paper, and formed the opinion it was very sound stuff. Gloomy times ahead, workshy buggers had better get used to the idea that there is no crock of gold waiting for them at the Pig and Whistle, everybody buckle to, get their heads down, and be damn grateful for their bread and dripping sandwiches. M. was opening the windows when I got back, and for want of anything better to say, I let fall words to the effect that Brother Pym seemed to have sounded the right note, must be music to her ears, clearly a good sort, very decent, plainly one of us, and not too stuck up like little Peter C. To my amazement I received a double-gamma burst from both eyes, and poor Pym was condemned in absentia to be strung up by the thumbs. When the dust had settled, Boris explained that the Icecreamio Twins from Saatchis had been in a few days previously, little Howe had brought his briefcase, and they'd cooked up some scheme for winning the election in 84, Luigi Saatchi urging that the talk from henceforth be all 'ultra-positive' and based on 'a good news hype' - bloody silly the way these admen go on - gentle take-off into miniboom, bulbs coming up, evenings getting longer, all the usual nonsense. Saatchis then took their money and buggered off. Pym not being privy to this wheeze, or so he claims, had thus incurred the proprietorial wrath, though if you ask me, Bill, she doesn't trust Pym much further than she can throw him and thinks he may be after her job. There was then the usual ritual dance: M. taxed by Worzel, leaps to feet in defence of Francis P., then scurries off to brief the reptiles, off the record of course, that she is hopping mad, Pym in doghouse etc. I shall never understand it.

If you ask me the Boss has got it all wrong. I don't know whether you remember when Maurice P. got into hot water with his chemical toilets workforce, i.e. those moronic darkies, all threatening to walk out. Maurice P. eschews encouraging words, spells out the grim message, moronic darkies all burst into tears and agree to take a pay cut. Of course the whole bang shoot fell in the water three days later so it didn't make a blind bit of difference, but my point is pretty clear I think.

So Brother Laker bites the dust. Good riddance in my view. I may have said this before, Bill, but it is high time the Hoi Polloi were booted out of airports, cluttering up as they do the entrance to the VIP lounge and littering the place with beercans.

Sorry you missed the Lillywhites Sale. I got a pair of those moonboots for when the snow comes back and a left-handed squash racket. Might come in useful one of these days, and very much reduced.

See you anon,

Yours aye,

DENIS

10 Downing Street

Whitehall

26 FEBRUARY 1982

Dear Bill,

Would you believe it? Some snotty-nosed Leftie MP had the gall to ask Margaret whether she would be picking up the tab for my little excursion to the Sahara last month, and now I get a bill from the Tamanrasset Hilton for £1893.95 including bar drinks and room service, which I am expected to pay. I knew the little Ali Baba chap was watering the gin and adding a pretty good mark-up, but assumed the Foreign Office would shell out come the day of reckoning. I have written to Mark asking for a contribution, but the day I get a penny back from that little skunk will be the day I sign the Pledge. Still, hats off to old Mitterand for paying the Mirage and helicopter fares.

So, our little midweek beanoes at the Club would seem to be at an end, that bloody fool Parker having caved in and given Buckton his three per cent with all the trimmings. What a prize prick, Bill! I have a feeling he used to be something in sugar with that dreadful man who lived near Henley, and I know there was some shemozzle about him driving a Rolls under poor old Callaghan, but I told the Boss she should give him his cards pronto and bring in some less smarmy type who might

be prepared to smack Buckton between the eyes and sort the whole thing out once and for all.

I can't understand - can you - all this sentimental tosh about the Laker man. I've said this before, and I'll probably say it again, but he has a lot to answer for in my view, cluttering up the departure lounges with the great unwashed, making it very difficult to get to the toilet on long-haul flights, and impossible to reach the bar for a drink when you arrive. Boss, on the other hand, has to don dark glasses to shield her eyes, such is the blaze of light beaming forth from Sir Frederick's arsehole. 'Good old Laker! Spirit of free enterprise, taking on the bully boys of Nationalised Industry, cutting the fares, pushing back the frontiers etc. etc.' After a bellyfull of this night after night I ventured to ask if she felt like that why didn't she step in and bale him out? Instant four megaton blast, exit DT with shirt tail smouldering. Anyway, the latest on the Laker Front, as you've probably gathered from the *Telegraph* is that Sir F has been fished out of the sewage by that Tiny Rowland cove. He seemed to me when I met him at the Guildhall rather a good sort, but the Major told me in confidence he is ninety nine per cent certain that he's a Kraut, his real name is Scharnhorst or something like that, and he may well have been Rommel's ADC in North Africa. Does that smell right to you? Anyway M. approves on the grounds that any enemy of E. Heath is a friend of hers.

So what else is new? Little Howe ponces in and out with increasing regularity to show Margaret his sums for next month's Day of Doom. Boris tried to break the combination lock on his briefcase while he was in the gents but it was fitted with some kind of buzzer device and Howe came flying out with his trousers round his ankles. There is a lot of talk though about bumping up the price of petrol yet again. It's a mystery to me, Bill. They've been banging on for years about the price of oil being the nigger in the woodpile, responsible for inflation and all our other woes, and the moment it starts coming down they throw up their hands in horror and start banging on the Purchase Tax. Fairly safe to assume that the Southern Comfort will be through the ceiling once again, ditto the Medium Tar, so could you do your usual re the Cash and Carry, and I'll get Maurice to send one of his darkies down with a pickup truck.

Yours up to here,

DENIS

10 Downing Street
Whitehall
12 MARCH 1982

Dear Bill,

Thank you for your PC. I agree with you one hundred percent about the Dirty Dozen cricketers in S. Africa. I knew nothing about it and neither did the Boss until it came up on the Jimmy Young Show while I was shaving. Boycott, we were told, along with Gooch and various other good men and true had surfaced in Johannesburg with their pads and cricket boots, all set for a few fixtures smiting the pill in the company of Brother Boer. I must say I could not forbear to let out a small cheer at the news. After all these years during which we have kowtowed to the darkies and Marxist Weirdoes here were our brave British lads hoisting the flag and putting the clock back to the good old days when they came over here and we went over there and no one gave a toss. As I may have said before, the Lefties as usual have got it all arse about face in that the last thing your average kaffir or Zulu Warrior wants to do is wield the willow, let alone spend all afternoon sitting in a deckchair watching the game. Besides which they are all too busy grubbing out the sparkling stone for White Bwana and in any case, according to the Major's friend Van der Vaal, now unfortunately inside for fraud, your black man just isn't properly coordinated for ball games. The West Indies is obviously another kettle of fish because apparently they're quite a different tribe. That's what Van der Vaal says, anyway.

My first impulse was to snatch up the blower and summon the Major to Stansted for immediate take-off. What better than a few days in the sun, dilatory applause trickling across the tree shaded ground and smartly dressed waiters with gleaming white teeth ferrying in the Pimms? But hardly had I dialled the number than the Boss came storming in saying had I heard the news about Boycott, why hadn't she been told, what was it all about? I ventured to present the case for the defence as outlined above, adding for good measure the usual stuff about Russian Ballet Dancers, but as so often when I think my words are about to strike a chord and two hearts will beat as one I was in for a cruel disappointment.

It turns out that M. has been taking a lot of stick from Mrs Gandhi and the Hordes, threatening the terminal twitch of the rug from under the Commonwealth if there is any more truck with the old Transvaal. Little Carrington has just been out to Rhodesia or whatever it's called nowadays, buttering up Mr Ebagum, despite the fact that he is turning out to be exactly what I always predicted, with Sticky's cousin and the Barltrop-Piries getting the hell out before the big massacre. At the time Peter C. wouldn't hear a word of this. Incidentally I thought General Haig rather got his number in the shiftiness department – 'duplicitous bastard' I felt hit the nail pretty solidly on the head, though it's obviously not a word you or I would ever use – but they all get their knickers in a knot when the word Commonwealth comes up on account of the Big White Mother in Buck House, who as I have told you before thinks Nyerere and Co are absolutely the Bee's Knees.

Otherwise the mood in the Fuehrer-bunker has been curiously euphoric. Saatchis have produced graphs to show that the SDP have peaked with the A/B share of the market and that Fatso will come a cropper in Glasgow. I know they always have to whistle to keep their spirits up, but I think they could be right on this one. I was talking to Maurice the other day about Alliance prospects in Sevenoaks, and I felt his heart had rather gone out of it. The local burghers seem very chary about stumping up his deposit and the Libs poured treacle over his steering wheel after the fund-raising Disco.

Talking of Libs, I was delighted to see that our friend Jeremy, clinging to the precipice by his finger tips while the Amnesty philanthropists stamped about on his knuckles with hobnailed boots, had finally relinquished his grip and disappeared into the abyss with a sickening shriek. Serve the little bugger right, in my view. I must say, if you or I were incarcerated in the Gulag it wouldn't do much for our spirits to be told that an old bum-bandit like Thorpe was lunching at the Reform on our behalf, trying to drum up a Round Robin to *The Times*.

I hope the shock of the Budget was somewhat cushioned by the tip I let you have about Amersham. That Lawson chap, normally a darn sight too oily for my liking, seemed to handle it very skilfully. I have always dinned into Margaret that we have to look after the Small Investor, like you and me.

A propos, Maurice has a new scheme for turning old copies of the *Daily Telegraph* into bricks, and suggests lunch later this month with a chap from Oslo who's patented the machine. Any chance of your joining us? I fear it may be rather a heavy session.

Yours till hell freezes over,

DENIS

10 Downing Street
Whitehall

26 MARCH 1982

Dear Bill,

Gripping days, what? We're all on tenterhooks here to see how Fatso Jenkins fares up in Glasgow. Saatchis, as you know, had written him off, but despite his girth and general shortage of wind, at the time of writing the old cove does seem to be making a last-minute dash for the tape.

God knows, our side have done their damnedest, and Howe's budget has been hailed on all sides as the first streaks of a new dawn, although quite honestly, Bill, it looks to me about as inky as inky black can get. I did a few sums on the talking calculator that Sticky brought back from Hong Kong, and I estimate that my own weekly expenditure on the very barest essentials, to wit snorts, gaspers and juice for the Rolls, has risen by 103% recurring.

They're all cock a hoop about interest rates coming down, but I pointed out to Howe that this is bad news for the Small Savers, such as yours truly, with his little nest-egg at the Natwest taking a very nasty knock. Furniss, our local manager, tried to soft soap me over a schooner or so of Amontillado that my deposit account still makes sense, but I told him if it was 11% to borrowers and 9% to savers, somebody was doing pretty damn well out of the missing two percent. That stopped him in his tracks, I don't mind telling you.

The black sheep of the week, I fear, is poor old Oyster Eyes. With every day that passes, more and more opprobrium is heaped upon his balding head. Boris blames the current rocketing in the crime figures on Margaret's unemployment policies, but that seems to me pretty good leftist drivel. I felt rather sorry for old Whitelaw, and ferried him down to Worplesdon in the Rolls the other afternoon, trying to spell out the views of the ordinary chap in the street. Was it any wonder, I opined over a large brownie in the Club before we set out into the March gale, that more and more criminals were at large in the community, accommodation no longer being available at any of Her Majesty's Prisons. Here was a gloriously simple way of killing two birds with one stone: scrap all these wishy washy apprentice schemes for mopping up the unem-

ployed youth, and set them to work building prisons up and down the land. Toxteth, Merseyside, Brixton. Whitelaw said there was one there already, but no matter. I pressed him to another large one and ploughed on. But as usual whenever I put forward a constructive suggestion, the old boy stood there with a glazed look, obviously thinking I was barking mad. Just as we were driving off from the first tee some bleeper thing went off in his pocket and his minder hurried him away to a waiting staff car, leaving DT trying to make up a foursome with the Battle of Britain mob.

No wonder the hangers and floggers are feeling pretty frustrated. I've a lot of sympathy with them, as you know. A good hanging never hurt anyone in my book, but what hope have they got with Oyster Eyes dithering about on the one hand, and the pissy-arsed little Euros on the other? If you can't even give some whipper-snapper in the fourth form six of the best without getting written approval from a lot of do-gooding Dutch bureaucrats, what hope of bringing back the noose, or flogging a bit of sense into Johnny Mugger? I line up with Enoch on this one, i.e. no jabbering Walloon or crop-headed Hun is going to tell us how to run the good ship SS Britain.

Talking of the Foreigner, I was pretty pissed off when you failed to turn up to the Club last week for lunch with Picarda's Danish Industrialist. Maurice had been there for a good couple of hours in my estimation, and the Dane, who I think I told you has invented a machine for recycling old copies of the *Daily Telegraph* for use as building bricks, had arrived the day before by mistake, and had been drinking ever since. Nice enough, and obviously full of jokes, but somewhat handicapped by not speaking a word of English. Maurice did his best with a word or two of German, and lunch was not by any means disagreeable, though the Head Waiter came over a couple of times to ask us to keep the noise down a bit for some bishops at the other end of the restaurant. About half way through, Jorg, as he asked me to call him, insisted on us toasting each other from a stone bottle containing some kind of colourless Danish sticky made from damsons, which Maurice and I found absolutely top-hole. If I could remember the name I'd order a crate of it, but I do recall a crown on the label and a black man playing a banjo, so I'd probably recognise it if I saw it again. Jorg then delved in his brief case and produced a sheet of coloured brochures showing smiling Danish housewives compressing the local equivalent of the *Daily Telegraph* and lots of little bricks ripening in the sun with views of the fjords thrown in for good measure. Maurice was absolutely bowled over by it all, and has agreed to set up a British subsidiary, Pickbrick. The long and the short of it is that I should take a pretty healthy slice of the equity with a seat on the board to follow. I must say I am seriously tempted by the idea, if only for the pleasure of seeing little Furniss's face when I tell him what he can do with his deposit account.

Hope you all had a good day at the Gold Cup. I lost a Monkey.

Yrs as per usual,

DENIS

10 Downing Street

Whitehall

9 APRIL 1982

Dear Bill,

I'm beginning to think I may have misjudged little Peter Carrington. When we first came in I took rather a shine to him: gent of the old school, not averse to the odd snorterino, the inevitable bit of side one expects from the Etonian brigade, but quite prepared to stand up to the Boss and trade blow for blow, unlike some of the other spineless creeps one sees slithering about the premises. Now I am beginning to hae me doots, as old McGargle would have put it.

I suppose the fact is that two or three years in politics, plus jet lag, having to talk to the Boss, booze round the clock etc. would drive anybody barmy. Be that as it may, you've probably heard on the wireless that there's some kind of rumpus blown up down in the South Atlantic, where there are a few inbred settlers left behind by various whalers over the years clinging to outcrops of guano-spattered rock, along with the odd sheep, reindeer and unhinged boffin. A state of affairs that has continued perfectly amicably for many centuries, until the excitable gauchos from el pampas across the water suddenly go bananas, letting off pistols, ole ole, and cry all

this is ours now. Though why they should want to take charge of these half-witted sheep-shaggers beats me.

When the balloon went up, the Boss got very excited, and pressed the intercom for P.C. pdq. Red faces at the F.O. P.C. it would appear A.W.O.L. buggering about on the Golan Heights trying to persuade Brother Begin to make room in the Promised Land for a couple of million dispossessed Wogs, an exercise about as pointless as trying to persuade Maurice or the Major to sign the Pledge. Why, you might enquire, would Carrington be thus engaged, apart that is, from the urge to enjoy a little Winterbreak among the olive groves? The answer of course is the Foreign Office's quite obscenely bumsucking attitude to the bearded sons of the desert on whose good will, we are told, our whole economy rests.

The real prick, I may say, is another Eton greaser called Hurd, who on this occasion was left minding the shop. He has also, according to Boris, just got spliced to some typist who is half his age, i.e. a D.O.M. to boot. Round he pops notwithstanding, to explain his master's absence at this time of crisis. I am glad to say the Boss administered a microwave attack that shrivelled him to cinders, and Carrington was told to abandon the skullcap routine and get his arse back to Whitehall where the safety of the sheep-shaggers hung perilously in the balance. Next thing — announcement on Jimmy Young Show that the invasion fleet has landed — balloon goes up: Parliament recalled for Saturday morning emergency session: high feeling the order of the day; even old Worzel waving the flag; many old buffers to whom Falkland Islands is just a name in the stamp album burst into tears. Long and the short of it is a slow motion replay of the Princes Gate show; give Brother Gaucho a bloody nose and little Nott haring about like a blue-arsed fly with the prospect of having to walk the plank at the end of the day if there's any kind of balls up.

As you will have gathered from the foregoing, Boss is on something of an up, what with Spring and so forth. The real reason, I suspect, is her habit of popping over to Brussels whenever things are looking a bit bleak on the domestic front, and bashing hell out of the nearest Frog. The louder they squeal the more she likes it, and returns to the H of C eyes agleam and cheeks touched with pink. The curious thing, though, as I have noticed from my perch in the Distinguished Drinkers' Gallery, is that old Worzel now looks at her through those pebble glasses of his with a funny leer that verges on respect, especially when she starts telling a few tall stories about her pugilistic encounters with the cauliflower-eared Brussels bruisers.

The other big excitement down at Halitosis Hall was the triumphant return of Fatso, fresh from his triumph in the Gorbals. According to Boris, the occasion was marred for our smooth-spoken friend by some Labour yobbo called Skinhead who bagged his seat, yelled a good deal of off-colour abuse at him, and forced the old gastronome to go and sit next to that frightful creep Freud, the dogfood man on the telly. I asked Saatchis, who were round the other morning for a post Hillhead rundown, how they fancied our chances now, and was given the usual head in the clouds guff about mid-term lag and hyping a turnaround, but Maurice is convinced that his hour has come at Sevenoaks and is banging on doors like a demented woodpecker.

Did you see Dougie Bader on *This Is Your Life*? I don't mind telling you I was blubbing like a baby and got through two bottles of your cash 'n carry hooch before the programme ended. Ah me, those were the days.

Is our Bank Holiday outing still on?

DENIS

P.S. Carrington has now done the decent thing. Clearly my words have had some effect.

10 Downing Street

Whitehall

23 APRIL 1982

Dear Bill,

I was very moved by your patriotic demonstration outside Number Ten the other evening. I hope you didn't think I was being stand-offish not coming out, but I always know when the Major in one of his argumentative moods, and hearing Maurice in such good voice in Rule Britannia, I deemed it best to acknowledge the ovation from an upper window. The Boss, entre nous, however chipper she may have appeared on the gogglebox, was not in the best frame of mind to receive spontaneous assurances of grass-roots support, even from such sober citizens as your good selves. I am sure you will understand.

I must say Hopalong has behaved like a prize twat over this one, and M. has made it pretty clear that the invitation to address the H of C may have to be drastically modified. Fancy sending over such an utter duffer as old Haig! I could tell from the moment I saw him blinking in the flashlights wearing that absurd tweed hat that the man wasn't all there up top, quite apart from the jetlag problem, and the various servicing requirements dictated by his clockwork heart pacer. Little Pym steered him into the manoeuvres room, and I did my best to make him feel at home with one of those American drinks with a bit of everything in, including tomato sauce and grated chocolate on top. He drank this at a draught, seemed rather perkier, and asked for another. His team of medicos, the Cardiac Brigade, five rather gloomy sawbones in black, looked somewhat askance, but I nonetheless obliged on humanitarian grounds, knowing he was in for a four hour bout with the Proprietor. I then withdrew to watch the snooker on the BBC.

From what I could hear through the door he rumbled on for a bit about the weather, but soon the Boss's shrill blast rose to hurricano level, harsh words were to be heard and what the FO wallahs call a full and frank exchange of views was clearly in progress. Being well fortified against these tempests, I think I may have nodded off, and the next thing I knew I was being hauled out to say goodbye for the benefit of the reptiles. Haig looked pretty badly mauled, and muttered something into the arclights about constructive new ideas, while Pym and the Boss looked on with acid gaze. Afterwards, while he was waiting for the taxi to take him back to the Air Terminal, Haig, assuming I think that I was Peter Carrington, R.I.P., suddenly focused on me, threw an arm round my shoulders, saying he couldn't understand why we'd taken against the Argies, nicest bunch of bastards he'd run up against in a long time, damn sound on Communism, a lot in common with the Boss when it came to knocking the shit out of old Brezhnev. I thought this mildly rum at the time, since according to Pym the Russkies are lining up with the Gauchos, but Pym might have got this wrong as he's after all new to the job. On reflection, however, it struck me, that Haig, absolute dunderhead though he may be, might after all have a point. Do you remember Batty Dugdale's funny uncle, Septimus, Arthur, some name like that? Run out of town with the Revenue men hot on his tail in the late forties, as I recall, set up in Argentina with a fancy ranch, breeding steers in a very big way to go into the Oxo Cubes. According to Batty who's been out there on and off over the years, Sidney or whatever he's called, the uncle, has a very agreeable style of life. No servant problem, tinctures on the verandah, extremely civilised existence, and so what if a blind eye is being turned to old Bormann and a few senile members of the Hitler Youth hiding out in the hills? We've sheltered some pretty odd people over here in our time. Look at the Tariq Ali man for instance. Not to mention Karl Marx holing up all those years in the British Museum when he was wanted by Interpol.

I'll tell you one very peculiar thing about it, Bill, and that is the Top Brass. I don't know whether you remember that rather pimply faced little subaltern who used to make up a four from time to time at Sandwich, can't remember his name, anyway, he's now C in C Combined Forces, and he was very chatty when M and I trailed round with Nott to raise morale.

I asked him who was actually in charge of the Fleet, the Nelson figure, shouting Fire Number One down the megaphone. It transpires it's not like that any more. Apparently there's this top secret hut near Virginia Water somewhere, with all the brass sitting round with Space Invader machines, waiting to press the tit at long distance. Just like Cape Canaveral when people go to the Moon: the Boffins do all the work, matelots only there to line up on deck and appeal to the cheering crowds, PR work, planting flags etc. It all sounds jolly odd to me, but as you're always saying, I'm just an old buffer, half plastered most of the time, but that's neither here nor there.

Where will it all end, you ask? On this point, the Saatchis are remarkably sanguine. In their view it'll be either (a) triumph, Argies pull down their blue and white rag and skulk back into their holes, or (b) total cock-up by our lot, national disaster. But this, they say, is just as good as (a) as far as M's popularity goes, British always keen on leaders in defeat, Gordon of Khartoum, Captain Scott, Dunkirk, Dieppe Raid. I asked them what happened if it just went on and on and on, with the Fleet sailing round in circles, Argies playing silly-buggers, Haig whizzing back and forth until like the legendary Oozlum Bird he vanishes up his own orifice? They obviously hadn't thought of that scenario, and looked pretty shifty.

Most extraordinary thing about it is Old Worzel's attitude. All those years stumbling about on the Aldermaston March, picking his nose at the Cenotaph, and now here he is, waving the flag and Up the Boss. I'm beginning to think that he may after all be one of us. When things have quietened down a bit perhaps we could ask the old boy out for a lunch at the RAC. What say you?

Yours for the duration,

DENIS